SELLING TECHNOLOGY

The Sandler Way

SELLING TECHNOLOGY
The Sandler Way

*Finding Technical Solutions That Win
Long-Term Business Relationships*

RICH CHIARELLO

Paperback: 978-0-9832615-9-9
E-book: 978-0-692-39529-5

This book is dedicated to my best friend, my wife Lorrie, who always believes in me and who shows me every day what it means to be strong; and to my daughter Tracy and my son Mike who remind me every day that even though I have made many mistakes in my life, I did find a way, with Lorrie's assistance, to provide the world with two truly great gifts.

Acknowledgments

I want to acknowledge David Mattson for seeing the reality of this book before I did; GuruGanesha Khalsa for introducing me to Sandler while I was running sales at Computer Associates; John Shrum for the fantastic coaching that helped me to turn the concepts between these covers into a business; Yusuf Toropov and Laura Matthews, who edited the manuscript; and Jerry Dorris, who laid the text out beautifully.

CONTENTS

FOREWORD xiii

CHAPTER 1: *Fifty Years to Create the Problem* 1

Why I Wrote This Book. 3

The More Things Change, the More
They Stay the Same. 5

Find the Business Problem. 7

Key Takeaways. . . . .,. . . .8

CHAPTER 2: *The Simple Math of Selling
in the Tech Space* 9

Begin at the Beginning. 9

What Needs to Happen for You
to Generate That Income? 10

Let's Play, "What If?" 12

Let's Play, "How Long?" 12

"Prove It!". 14

My Challenge to You 16

Key Takeaways. 17

CHAPTER 3: *Product Knowledge—Use It or Lose It?* 19

   A Question. 20

   Think Back 21

   The Landmine. 22

   Discipline. 24

   The Right Way to Use Product Knowledge 25

   Find the Reason 27

   Key Takeaways. 29

CHAPTER 4: *What Is Your Value Proposition?* 31

   Who's Your Target? 33

   A Familiar Example 34

   Find the Value Proposition of the Features 36

   Where Do You Want to Invest Your Time? 37

   Key Takeaways. 39

CHAPTER 5: *Dealing with Prospecting Reluctance* 41

   Moving Beyond the Comfort Zone 42

   Why Head Trash Happens 45

   Removing the Head Trash. 46

   Key Takeaways. 48

CHAPTER 6: *The Stress-Free Sales Call* 49

   The Pattern Interrupt. 52

   The 30-Second Commercial. 53

   The Up-Front Contract 54

   Fishing for Pain. 56

   Close for the Appointment 57

   Post-Sell the Appointment 58

   It Works—in High-Tech and Everywhere Else 59

   Key Takeaways. 60

CHAPTER 7: *Diagnosis or Treatment?* 61

(Mis)Diagnosis 63

Symptom or Problem? 65

Key Takeaways 70

CHAPTER 8: *Pain Is the Best Impending Event!* 71

A Solution to the Problem 72

Do They Want Your Solution as Much
    as You Want the Sale? 74

Moving beyond the Discount 76

Key Takeaways 81

CHAPTER 9: *Selling to the Stakeholders* 83

How Many Stakeholders? 84

Are They Qualified for Decision? 86

Identify the Cast 88

Assume Nothing! 89

Get Multiple Information Sources 90

DISC 91

One on One 95

Off the Org Chart 96

Key Takeaways 101

CHAPTER 10: *All Prospects Are Not Created Equal* 103

Abundance 104

The "Budget" Issue 107

The "Who's Leading This Dance?" Issue 107

Seller Beware 109

Qualifying, for Real, with the Mutual Action Plan 110

"My Biggest Fear" 111

Key Takeaways 113

CHAPTER 11: *Handling Objections.* 115

    Handling the Anxiety 117

    What's the Real Objection? 119

    Defuse the Emotion 120

    Key Takeaways. 125

CHAPTER 12: *More on Mutual Action Plans* 127

    Key Takeaways. 134

EPILOGUE. 135

FOREWORD

As a sales professional, you face special challenges when you sell technical solutions whose inner workings end users not only don't understand, but don't particularly want to understand.

Not infrequently, these solutions are deployed across larger, more complex organizations. The possibility of their adoption is likely to affect influential people across multiple constituencies. Typically, these players have competing interests, and some of them are likely to be committed to preventing consensus from emerging around your offering. You may even find yourself selling into an environment where there are "invisible" stakeholders: individuals who don't show up on anyone's org chart. And, of course, you may run into competition, entrenched and otherwise, that is better funded and better connected than you are.

These are, in short, dangerous waters. To navigate them

successfully, it helps to have a guide who knows the waters well. You need someone with an accurate map you can use to get from where you are now to where you want to go. You need someone who has direct experience piloting a big ship from its starting point to its final destination. Last but not least, you need someone who already knows where the trickiest hidden obstacles to your voyage's success are.

The Sandler Selling System is the map, and Rich Chiarello is an expert guide. He knows these waters well. His book is a major contribution to salespeople who sell technical solutions, and it is an honor for us to share the insights he has gathered between these covers.

—David H. Mattson
President and CEO, Sandler Training

CHAPTER 1

Fifty Years to Create the Problem

In the early 1960s, global technology companies (led by United States giants such as IBM and Xerox) began turning the industrial creativity of their workforces toward information-management products that could be consumed by corporations. They didn't realize it at the time, but they were setting up a crisis—for themselves and all their current and future competitors.

The technology innovations began with the vacuum tube, followed by the transistor, followed by the circuit chip. The trend toward smaller and more efficient management of data created a tidal wave of electronic inventions that saved labor and thereby greatly increased personal and organizational efficiency.

These strange new machines produced explosions in productivity. People used them to run prebuilt programming (software), which, when combined with the physical platform, delivered even greater efficiencies for institutions—and also created certain organizational and personal expectations. Staff wanted simpler and simpler solutions when it came to data management, but they understood less and less about how those solutions were designed, how they worked or how they fit together.

This new way of looking at technology was (and is) revolutionary. Most end users never even consider trying to figure out how their gadgets work internally. The design and engineering that goes into technology solutions on which we have all become dependent remains in the hands of the experts. It was not always this way.

When I was in my twenties, I changed the oil, oil filter, sparkplugs and so on for all my cars. If something went wrong with a timing belt or a carburetor, I prided myself on my ability to fix it. Today, there's no such thing as a carburetor for me to fix. When car troubles arise, I open the hood and stare at the machinery just long enough to satisfy my ego. I then gently close the hood and call for a tow truck. If you're like most of the people I meet, you do, too.

That instinct to call the tow truck instead of troubleshooting the car's computer system is how we live today. Notice the trend: Simpler and simpler solutions for the end user requiring greater and greater design complexity are accompanied by less and less understanding (or interest) from the end user about the specifics of how everything actually works "under the hood."

This trend is unstoppable. It is visible throughout our culture. Of course, it is also simultaneous with the rise of high-tech. If you doubt that, ask yourself these questions:

- When it's time to upgrade your smartphone, do you expect the newest model to do more or less than your current one?

- But do you know, or even care, how your smartphone works?

I call this trend "end-user/feature disengagement." You, I and all the other end users of technology in the world are strongly predisposed not to care about the features and specifications of the information products we use. This trend is only growing stronger. It is unstoppable.

> ### SANDLER TIP
> *You, I and all the other end users of technology in the world are strongly predisposed not to care about the features and specifications of the information products we use.*

WHY I WROTE THIS BOOK

The purpose of this book is to look pragmatically at the effects of end-user/feature disengagement, not so much for the consumer who uses the tools and platforms we associate with the tech space, but for the sales teams eager to improve their performance in the marketplace.

I'm talking specifically about sales teams in small, medium and large businesses tasked with making a living and turning a profit by selling those tools and platforms. Most sales teams are burdened with a features-driven selling model that is outdated in all markets—and practically suicidal in this one.

To understand why this is so—why so many companies in the high-tech space continue to follow a process that is dangerously out of step with how people in their target market buy—you have to understand something unique about the high-tech space.

Over the last five decades or so, all the companies in this space— whether they were small, large or somewhere in-between—had one thing in common. They were all technology companies with products created by technicians in engineering labs. That meant that the products tended to manifest themselves in the form of spec sheets and complex technical descriptions that were then handed down to both marketing and sales departments.

Companies did this for what seemed (at the time) very good reasons. They thought they needed to operate this way so that marketing could find leads and sales could sell. But in the end, this resulted in the sales department cultures of many, many successful enterprises being based on product knowledge.

Stating this selling culture in a single sentence would sound something like this: "If I can pin you down long enough for you to let me educate you on my product, you will discover a feature that I have that you need to buy."

That's called trying to sell from your knowledge base. It is death in today's market.

Yet most high-tech salespeople still try to sell this way, even though the people they're selling to are not tech people—with zero tech background or interest in features.

THE MORE THINGS CHANGE, THE MORE THEY STAY THE SAME

When it comes to sales, not much has changed in the tech space since the 1970s. Sure, the buzzwords are different. We now think of what was once called "time sharing" of computer resources very differently; today, we think of that as a service. We are now more likely to think of "mobile solutions" than we are about "client/server" applications.

> ### SANDLER TIP
>
> *Salespeople and sales teams who overachieve in the years to come will be the technology "midwives," the translators who know that educating the consumer is not where the sales process begins—in high-tech or anywhere else.*

The changes will continue. The buzzwords we use today will all be different a few years from now. But the one thing all the buzzwords will have in common is this: they will be inventions that start out in engineering departments and create a "trickledown" of spec sheets and complex features descriptions. This verbiage will eventually make its way into the hands of the business development and sales teams. Those teams will then have to figure out how to create engaging conversations with prospects without sounding like physics professors.

The salespeople and sales teams who overachieve in the years to come will be the ones who are able to listen to a technological explanation of some solution—and then be ready, willing and able to translate the technical capabilities of the product into the business outcomes it provides and/or the problems it resolves.

This is no secret; it's just widely ignored. It is widely ignored in the tech space today, and it was widely ignored years ago. Every once in a while, back in the day, you might run into someone who knew the key to overachieving in this space. When I started out at IBM selling large-scale mainframe systems, a particular sales visit was followed by what would turn out to be a very instructive debrief with my sales manager on our way back to the office. I thought I had totally impressed the prospect with my newly acquired knowledge of our products. But my sales manager calmly told me that if I was bound and determined to educate people about IBM computers or anything else, sales was the wrong career for me.

SANDLER TIP

Great salespeople in the high-tech space know how to ask questions, collect data, and "diagnose" based on good information.

Half joking, he asked me whether I might be better off being a college professor or a tour guide at the Vatican! That was the first time I was told that success on my sales calls would be measured by how much information I collect, not by how much I distribute.

FIND THE BUSINESS PROBLEM

Much like a great doctor who doesn't bore you with the "how I know what's wrong with you" explanations or what he has learned during his decades of training, great salespeople in the high-tech space know how to ask questions, collect data and "diagnose" based on good information. They don't tell their prospects how the vaccines are made. They figure out whether the prospect has a fever they can cure. That's not all they do. They also understand the value of their solution, not only to their individual customers, but to the organizations for which those customers work. Most likely, the greatest salespeople in the high-tech space of the next decades will be trained by Sandler. This book gives you an overview of what they will practice.

KEY TAKEAWAYS

- Most high-tech firms still operate under a system whereby products manifest themselves in the form of spec sheets and complex technical descriptions that are then handed down to both marketing and sales departments.

- Most end users, however, don't care about features or spec sheets.

- The salespeople and sales teams who overachieve in the years to come will be the technology "midwives"—the translators who know that educating the consumer is not where the sales process begins.

- Great salespeople in the tech space know how to identify business problems they can help solve and what to ask the prospect to identify whether there is a realistic possibility of finding a solution together.

CHAPTER 2

The Simple Math of Selling in the Tech Space

Most salespeople are motivated to change (or not) in the same way the buyers are motivated to take action—Pain. They need some encouragement because they're not yet certain why they should invest time in learning about the Sandler Selling System or change their approach to selling. This chapter provides that nudge. It's specifically designed for people who sell in the tech space and whose prime motivational factor (pain) is making money.

BEGIN AT THE BEGINNING

Let's start with two basic propositions upon which everyone— you, me, your sales manager and your loved ones who are counting on you to succeed—can all agree. First, there is such a thing as a closing ratio. Second, you have one right now.

In other words, out of the pool of people you consider to be qualified prospects, some percentage is being closed by you right now. For the purposes of this chapter, I'm going to assume that number, whatever it is, reflects your closing activity over a significant period of time—say, the past twelve months.

Whenever I'm working with groups, I ask them to arbitrarily pick a number that reflects a typical closing ratio in their company. Let's say that number is two out of every ten people. That means you sell to two out of every ten accounts you consider to be qualified prospects. You and I might disagree about what constitutes a qualified prospect, but we're going to let that go for the moment. For the sake of argument, let's assume that everyone you deem to be qualified is in fact a qualified prospect.

Let's say that closing ratio, two out of ten, is currently delivering $200,000 a year to you as a salesperson. The lower your average sales price and the more transaction-oriented your role, the greater the size of these metrics. Divide $200,000 by your average deal's commission, and this will tell you about how many deals you need to close to maintain that amount.

WHAT NEEDS TO HAPPEN FOR YOU TO GENERATE THAT INCOME?

Let's say that in order to generate ten live prospects, in all likelihood you have to talk to something like 50 "suspect" people/

accounts. (Again, I'm not saying that these numbers are literally accurate—they're just in the ballpark of what most salespeople we work with in the tech sector experience.)

In order to talk to those 50 people, it's likely that you have to make something like 20–30 phone calls a day if you are in enterprise or account sales (40–60 if you are in telesales), week in, week out, every working day. That number may seem high, but remember that it includes callbacks, people who don't answer and repeat dials. If you're like most of the salespeople we know, you must maintain that high volume on a daily basis. If you're lucky, ten of the people you reach out to by phone will want to continue the discussion with you.

Of course, continuing the discussion isn't really what you're after. You're after in-depth discussions with decision makers— discussions that take up multiple visits and involve multiple points of contact within the organization. The numbers tell us that you need a total of 30 of those kinds of in-depth contacts over the course of the year to make your commission. We've said too that you're likely to close two out of ten, or six total deals. That adds up to $200,000 (or much higher after you completed the prior paragraph's formula).

This is just one scenario, involving a fairly high dollar value for each deal. But it is a realistic scenario for people working in the tech center. With me so far?

Good. Let's keep going.

LET'S PLAY, "WHAT IF?"

Whenever good salespeople set up their sales plan for the year, they try to estimate how much money they're going to make over that twelve-month period. That's the whole point of the exercise. You've probably done the same thing for your current year.

I want you to take whatever that number is and hold it in your mind. It might be lower or higher than $200,000. Ask yourself this question: "What would I buy and how would my lifestyle change if I were able to increase that number by 50 percent?" Instead of making $200,000, as in our example, let's say you made $300,000. What would you do?

Would you buy a car? A couple of cars? A fleet of motorcycles? Maybe put a down payment on a new house? Or pay off some loans? Or would you go on a longer, more satisfying vacation than last year?

I need you to come up with a clear answer to this question—it's very important!—and I need you to be able to visualize that answer. This part of the book is up to you to fill in. I can't do this part for you. All I can do is ask you to have a clear picture of that new lifestyle in your mind before you move on to the next step.

What if you could double that expected number—i.e., $400,000? Do I have your attention?

LET'S PLAY, "HOW LONG?"

Now take a moment to think about how many years you have left in your career as a salesperson. Make a realistic estimate.

Based on your age, it might be ten more years, it might be 20, it might be 30. Pick the right number.

> ## SANDLER TIP
>
> *Sandler has helped thousands of people increase their income just by putting into action the principles you'll learn about in this book.*

Got it? Good. Now figure out what you can do with all of that money, over the course of all of those years. How different would your life be if you had 50–100 percent more income to work with, each and every year, from now until the end of your career?

How frustrated are you today that others make that kind of money?

What have you done to fix this inequity?

How did that work?

How did that make you feel?

Have you given up, and are you willing to accept this as fact?

—Or—

Would you like to do something about this situation?

By now, perhaps you are thinking something like this: "It sounds great, Rich—but how are you going to back it up? How realistic is it that I'm going to be able to earn 50–100 percent more than I thought I would over the next twelve months? Does anyone actually do that?"

The answer is "yes."

What I'm proposing is quite realistic. In fact, Sandler has helped tens of thousands of salespeople increase their income by 50–100 percent just by putting into habitual action the principles you'll learn about in this book.

"PROVE IT!"

Here is the simple math of the sales formula:

$$\$ = QPR \times C\%$$

QPR = the revenue represented by your qualified prospects,
and C% = close percentage

Think of it this way: Assume you're currently closing two out of every ten prospects, and you believe, deep in your heart, that you can't work any harder or any smarter than you already are. That's fair.

If, by using the Sandler® methodology, you did nothing but get twice as good at qualifying as you are right now, you could realistically expect to move from closing two out of every ten prospects to closing four out of every ten prospects within just 90–120 days.

Yes, that works out to an increase of 100 percent in your commission income. We've seen that happen hundreds of times. It can happen for you.

Here's where we have to ask you to give Sandler Training some credit. Do you think we're not going to give you *anything* to improve your sales skills beyond the qualifying phase, nor help you to increase the revenue represented by your QBR?

SANDLER TIP

Even if you only improved your qualifying skills by implementing what you will find here, that would have a powerful, positive effect on your income.

We're not even talking yet about improvements in your income resulting from getting better at interviewing or becoming more effective at closing. With improvements in those areas, can you imagine what you could accomplish? What kinds of changes could you make in your life?

We have seen plenty of people move from closing two out of ten to closing six out of ten. If you think a 60 percent closing ratio is unrealistic in this industry, then you're the person for whom I wrote this book.

Ask yourself this one question: If you stopped calling all of your qualified prospects, how many would pick up the phone and call you first? All those who would not call you do not feel that they need to buy from you as much as you feel you need to sell to them.

MY CHALLENGE TO YOU

That's the simple math of selling in the tech space. My challenge to you now is to keep reading—and to put into action the advice you find on the following pages. Try what I suggest. See for yourself whether your numbers start moving in the right direction.

KEY TAKEAWAYS

- If, by using the Sandler methodology, you did nothing more than get twice as good at qualifying as you are right now, you could realistically expect to move from closing two out of every ten prospects to closing four (or even six) out of every ten prospects, thereby possibly doubling (or tripling) your sales, within just 90–120 days.

- If you also increased your sales skills by 50 percent, you would now be closing sales with 2.5 times improvement over where you are today.

- This increase in sales and subsequent commissions will span your lifetime.

CHAPTER 3

Product Knowledge— Use It or Lose It?

L et's start with a reality that no successful salesperson in high-tech that I've ever met would dispute. It is difficult to succeed in the world of high-tech sales without at least a basic working understanding of both your company's complex solution and how it may or may not solve the prospect's complex problem.

Having acknowledged that much, though, I want to suggest that we need to address another reality, one that is sometimes a little more difficult for salespeople to process. It sounds like this: Sometimes, the very product knowledge that we need in order to conduct intelligent discussions with prospects can become one of the biggest obstacles to our own success.

In chapter two, we looked at the first parameter for expanding your income as a salesperson: increasing the number of conversations that you have with qualified prospects. In this chapter, we will focus on a deeper question, namely: How does product knowledge degrade the quality of conversations you have with prospects by reducing your ability to fully qualify prospects for your solutions? And, we won't leave out what you should do instead!

SANDLER TIP

Sell today. Educate tomorrow.

A QUESTION

Ask yourself this question: "When I am qualifying a prospect, who is usually the first to be convinced that there's a deal—the prospect or me?"

Often, I find it is overly eager salespeople who have the greatest issues with the over-use of product knowledge. Every time they talk to a prospect, they convince themselves of one of two things: "This prospect is qualified to buy; let me start the education process," or "If I show this prospect all the wonders of my solution, he will magically become qualified and want to buy from me."

This is delusional thinking, usually triggered by something like an earlier request for product information from the prospect. Whenever the overeager salesperson hears that, a round of premature feature-selling usually follows. Generally, it doesn't end well.

THINK BACK

Let me invite you to consider your own sales career for a moment. If you're like a lot of the salespeople we work with, you had a period of relatively easy early success with your current company, followed by a pronounced drop off. For some people, that happens in a very compressed timeframe; for others it takes longer to play out. But that pattern is very common. Perhaps it's a familiar one to you.

Why did it happen, in your case? Think back. Does any explanation come to mind?

Try this on for size. When you first started selling for your current company, you most likely did not know all that much about the solutions you were supposed to sell. You were forced, for practical reasons, to find some way to get the prospect to do most of the talking, simply because your own knowledge of your products was limited. By default, you were putting the spotlight on the prospect. That led you to uncover important information—information that eventually led you toward sales.

Then what happened? As your tenure with your current firm increased, so did your knowledge of both the solutions your company offered and the other solutions competing with you in the marketplace. You had more to discuss. You took advantage of your product knowledge as an opportunity to show prospects how much you knew. For many of us, this became the most self-satisfying part of our job. We began to move off the prime objective—qualifying prospects—and found a more self-fulfilling goal—the prospect's admiration for our product knowledge. This of course made us subconsciously seek out similar situations so that we could again feel good about ourselves. It also led to a lot of "free consulting" and many sales cycles with unqualified prospects.

> ### SANDLER TIP
> *Most people would rather talk about themselves and their issues than listen to someone else expound his knowledge.*

Even though you did it by accident, you were following a basic Sandler Selling System® principle in the early portion of your time with your company. You were making sure that the customer did the vast majority of the talking. But as you got to know more and more about all the various solutions, you started to talk more and more. That made it more and more difficult for you to uncover the information you needed to close the sale. And, your income dropped.

Does any of what you just read sound at all familiar, either in regard to you or in regard to someone you know who sells in the high-tech space?

THE LANDMINE

When I started at IBM as a pre-sales systems engineer, you could have put what I knew about computers on the back of a stamp.

Up to that point, I had never engineered anything bigger than my Lionel trains. When I met customers who had no idea of my industry knowledge void, I had no alternative but to ask them about their systems, needs and desires. This worked out pretty well, since most people would rather talk about themselves and their issues versus listen to someone else expound his knowledge. I became one of the most sought-after pre-sales resources by the sales teams. Over the next two years, I did get trained in large-scale computer systems and operating systems and did the entire installation for my clients on my own. I astounded myself at what IBM was able to teach me.

Then one day a sales manager asked me if I would like to move into sales. Aside from my wanting to make more money, he astutely realized I'd be motivated by something else as well. As someone who scored highest on the "I" and "D" profiles of the DISC behavioral assessment, I had a choice to make. I could work extremely hard at being a systems engineer but never be any better than a "B" player, or I could use my natural skills in sales and have a much more rewarding career. You guessed it—I chose the sales road.

So I found that I knew more about how computers worked than even the most senior salespeople. This was a big problem! On sales calls, I started to feel good when people complimented me on what I knew instead of when I could qualify a prospect into or out of my pipeline. I would ask maybe one or two qualifying questions to see if the company had a problem. But if the prospect answered, "That could be something in which we might be interested. How would you solve that for us?" I would go right into my core dump of product knowledge. Instead, I should always have probed more for the business and personal issues underlying that answer. Additionally, I should have explored what "we may be interested" meant to the prospect. Alas, I stepped on the knowledge landmine. I became Professor Chiarello.

Right now, your product knowledge almost certainly represents a greater risk to your success than it did when you first started out. Why? Because you are, in all likelihood, not using that knowledge effectively. You're using it to show off. You're a tour guide at the Vatican.

In my experience, the single biggest sales landmine that salespeople detonate is the mistake of allowing their product knowledge to tempt them into either selling too soon or allowing their ego to control the sales call. In both cases, they give out much more information than they receive. That's a big mistake.

DISCIPLINE

In order to increase the amount of time we spend with qualified prospects, we must have a much more disciplined process—one that delays the point at which we start selling until after the prospect has been fully qualified.

This word "qualified" is worth examining closely. It probably means more than you think it means. In Sandler parlance, "qualified" means, not just that the person could conceivably choose to buy and use our solution at some point in time, but is at the point of sale in terms of the Pain, Budget and Decision Steps of the Sandler selling process.

It's always useful to look closely at the Pain Step as well.

Within that step, we as salespeople need to identify both the business pain and the personal pain that connects to this buyer. We need to do that prior to our investing significant amounts of time with that person. Most high-tech salespeople—in fact, most salespeople, period—violate this rule.

If, early in the conversation, the prospect asks us why our hammers are better than our competitors' hammers, we run the risk of stepping on a landmine. With too much product knowledge and too little discipline, we might start articulating how many different hammers we have for sale and why each of them is the very best in the market. What we probably should say, though, is, "May I ask you what makes you think you need a hammer?"

Remember, sales is not the place you go to get your own personal needs met. If being admired for your product knowledge makes you feel better about yourself at that moment, great. But I guarantee you the good feeling will not last because it will not move your sales needle in the right direction.

THE RIGHT WAY TO USE PRODUCT KNOWLEDGE

By now, you're probably asking yourself, "How should I use my product knowledge?" The answer is pretty simple. Product knowledge should be used like a good physician uses the knowledge he accumulated in medical school.

Think about it. It takes many years of study to become a doctor. Once the doctor begins practicing, he applies appropriate knowledge to patients—how? Not by delivering long lectures, but by being a good diagnostician.

Good salespeople in the high-tech space do much the same thing. They know how to match the capabilities of their products with the appropriate business problems they have diagnosed—problems they know they can solve for the prospect. Albert Einstein once said, "Imagination is more important than knowledge." Truly great salespeople use product knowledge imaginatively, in ways that help both themselves and the prospect picture what life would be like using their solution.

The process for matching features and problems is straightforward. Start with the features that are most valuable in your solution, then determine what business problems those features solve. Ask yourself: What symptoms might a prospect's business have with those particular business problems? The final step is to put together what questions you would ask a prospect to see whether those symptoms are present.

In the same way the physician uses the symptoms of high temperature, elevated blood pressure, coughing and so forth to understand what solution, if any, is needed for the patient, the successful salesperson performs diagnostics on the prospect prior to investing any significant sales time. How? By asking questions. These questions are used to get the prospect to open up with regard to what problem needs to be solved, how that problem is affecting the organization and how it affects the prospect as an individual.

But there's a problem. Since most prospects tend to have a comfort zone around listening and not divulging information, and since most salespeople have a comfort zone around delivering information and not asking questions that require the salesperson to listen, the deck would seem to be stacked against sales. You need to make a conscious effort to step out of your comfort zone. In this book, I'll be sharing a number of tools that will help you to do that, along with helping you to ensure that the prospect does 70–80 percent of the talking.

Here's why you should move outside your comfort zone: Your commission check is usually directly linked to how much information you obtain, as opposed to how much you deliver, during a sales call.

FIND THE REASON

It is much more important to understand why the prospect asked a certain question than it is to answer it. Think about it. Whatever the prospect asked you, there must have been a good reason for that to be the first or second or third question. You need to understand what those reasons are.

An attendee at one of our classes said that he wanted to know how to apply Sandler principles in dating. Something weird had happened the prior night in a bar. He had been having a delightful conversation with a young lady whom he just met. Twenty minutes into the conversation, she asked, "Are you married or single?" He asked me, "Why would she ask me that question? Do I look like I am married?"

I told him that Sandler teaches that it is always about the prospect. I guaranteed him that the reason this question was asked so early is that it represented a pain point. Either she or a close friend had had a bad experience dating a married man, so this became her first question when meeting people. There is usually a pain point behind prospects' first questions. You need to focus on why they are asking it rather than how smart you can appear by providing the answer.

Successful salespeople know that behind these reasons lies the information necessary to either qualify or disqualify the prospect for the privilege of our valuable selling time.

KEY TAKEAWAYS

- Sometimes, the very product knowledge that we need in order to conduct intelligent discussions with prospects can become one of the biggest obstacles to our own success.

- Sales is not the place for you to get your personal needs met.

- It is more important to understand why a question was asked then it is to provide the prospect with the answer.

CHAPTER 4

What Is Your Value Proposition?

One reliable way to ensure that you increase the number of conversations you have with qualified prospects and to decrease those with unqualified prospects is to have a firm understanding of the value proposition for your product or solution.

What does that mean? It means you need to understand exactly what business problems your solution solves, what types of companies and people most often have these problems and what symptoms are most likely to manifest themselves to the companies and people who struggle with these problems. Using a set of pain-probing questions early in your conversations with prospects, you can identify whether these problems exist in that person's world. (You'd be surprised how many salespeople in the tech field don't do any of those things.)

SANDLER TIP

If everyone is a prospect, then no one is a prospect.

In my experience, too many marketing and sales organizations try to cast too wide a net into the marketplace. Too many salespeople delude themselves into believing that everyone is a prospect for their solution. The reality is that if we make everyone into a prospect, no one is truly a prospect. What you need to understand is: What are the characteristics of your ideal prospect?

David Sandler, the founder of Sandler Training, said: "Selling is what takes place when you lead the prospect through a step-by-step process, each step of which may lead to the prospect's disqualification and removal from the process. If you do not disqualify the prospect opportunity, the sale moves forward, and eventually culminates in the prospect making a buying decision."

The ideal prospect is someone who is willing to engage with you and take action—someone who is willing to work with you as a partner. Look at your own history, your own interactions with the people who became your very best customers. I'm willing to bet you'll find that it was only certain people—the ideal prospects—who had a sense of shared urgency and investment during the sales cycle, who signed off on mutual action plans and who maintained communication with you all the way through the process. Why? Because you had a clear solution that fit their problem very closely. As a result, these people not only "played ball" with you as the sales process moved forward, they often paid a premium price for your solution, since they did not view it as a commodity.

Understanding your own value proposition means knowing who your ideal prospects are and what outcomes they are most likely to want.

WHO'S YOUR TARGET?

Let's use restaurants as an example. If I were going to open up a new establishment in my town, I would need to understand what I could do best and then decide on what type of audience my new cuisine would attract. A McDonald's or Burger King audience is typically people who are looking for inexpensive meals with fast service and a family orientation. On the other hand, a high-end restaurant that features a five-star chef would appeal to a completely different target audience. Even though I'm selling food in both cases, trying to target "everyone in town" wouldn't get me very far.

Check this out for yourself. The next time you go out to dinner, ask the owner or manager about it. Successful restaurant owners know from their own personal experience that no one restaurant can appeal to all tastes all the time. Those that have tried typically have gone out of business in short order. Why? Because they hadn't ever excelled in any one area of the marketplace. Restaurants that succeed know who their ideal customer is. It's the same for salespeople.

Nowhere is the answer to, "Who would make the best prospect for my product?" more important than in technology sales.

It often takes prospects several months of the sales cycle to disqualify themselves as they learn more about your solution, the problems that it solves and the associated costs. Good salespeople recognize this issue and accept it as a reality of selling in their industry. As a result, they do not rely on prospects to disqualify themselves from a sales cycle. Good salespeople know that a far greater percentage of prospects will turn out to be disqualified, rather than qualified. Consequently, they have learned to hold back on selling until they can confirm in their own minds why it would make sense for the prospect to invest money, time, attention and political capital in their solution.

SANDLER TIP

Good salespeople know that a far greater percentage of prospects will turn out to be disqualified, rather than qualified.

A FAMILIAR EXAMPLE

Let's prove this in a high-tech example that will be familiar to just about everyone. When the Apple iPhone was first introduced, it initially sold for around $700. The competition was selling for about $99, or in many cases at no charge, if the person committed to a two-year telephone plan.

Now, if Apple had viewed "everybody who needs a cell phone" as their target audience, they would have wasted a lot of time, energy and marketing dollars going after people who would never have participated in the early adoption phase. Rather, they understood that their target audience was people who wanted to be ahead of the curve and who would appreciate having email, full-screen Internet browsing, a camera and their favorite songs all in one device—even though no one had ever had all that before. Additionally, Apple's version of the ideal prospect was someone who was already committed to a mobile email device such as a Blackberry and therefore was already experiencing the cost of this technology and the inconvenience of needing multiple devices.

Guess what? If you look back on all of the early advertisements from Apple, they were clearly targeted to this audience. Those ads were all designed to heighten the targeted audience's pain state. They were quite effective, too!

When Steve Jobs introduced the iPhone in 2007 on stage, his words were, "A widescreen iPod with touch controls, a revolutionary mobile phone and a breakthrough Internet communication device."

Remember, too, the state of affairs when the iPhone was launched. The main problem it solved was the need to carry multiple devices. The status quo represented both a major cost (the need to pay for multiple devices) and major inconvenience (multiple chargers, remembering to take all the devices). People who experienced those costs and that inconvenience were Apple's ideal prospects. The symptoms of these needs were pretty obvious to those of us who traveled in airports during that time. You may remember seeing people using Blackberries for email and PCs for Internet browsing and looking for multiple places to charge their devices. Maybe you were one of those people! (I was.)

So if your name was John and you worked for Apple at the time, what would your 30-Second Commercial have sounded like? It might have sounded like this:

> Hi, my name is John and I work for Apple. We are a leading provider of business productivity devices. People like you are switching away from their current mobile email device and going with the iPhone because they are frustrated over the amount of devices they need to carry for email, the Internet, picture taking and their music; they're annoyed at the small screen provided for Internet browsing on their current device or challenged by the difficulty in using all of these devices. Are any of these a concern for you?

FIND THE VALUE PROPOSITION OF THE FEATURES

Notice that the above was not a list of the iPhone's features: the battery life, the components from which it was constructed, the specs for the screen, or anything like that. Of course, if you were John, you would need to know about all that. But all that stuff wouldn't be the value proposition you shared with people who might turn into prospects. The value proposition connects to the pain, and that's what John's 30-second commercial is built around.

You can do exactly what Apple did. By knowing what features of your solution are most valuable to prospects, you can identify the problems they solve and then the symptoms these problems manifest in your ideal prospects. You can then create the probing, qualifying pain questions you need to start good sales conversations. It's a very simple equation. That equation is what allows you to charge $700 for a new piece of technology, while the competition is going for a fraction of that!

WHERE DO YOU WANT TO INVEST YOUR TIME?

With whom would you rather start a sales cycle: someone who may need some of your features but could do with an alternate solution, or someone who needs what your product does best and most likely will be unable to find anywhere else?

Who do you think will pay you more in the end?

If you want to see how this process would work with the solution that you are selling, complete the following chart.

Feature	Benefit	Pain Indicator	Question I Ask

Take the three most powerful features of your solution and put those in column one. Then complete each line moving from left to right, outlining the business benefit of the feature, the pain indicator or "symptom" that the prospect would typically have and the question that you would ask to see if the symptom was present.

KEY TAKEAWAYS

- Understanding your own value proposition means knowing who your ideal prospects are and what outcomes they are most likely to want.
- Qualify prospects by asking if they have the problems that your solution solves.
- Since mathematically most initial conversations do not turn into prospects, you should be looking hard for the reasons to qualify a prospect. Start from the position that he is probably not qualified.

CHAPTER 5

Dealing with Prospecting Reluctance

I n their heart of hearts, most salespeople recognize that their existing contacts within an account represent only a small portion of the potential buyers within their territory. The question is, what do you do with that information?

The first step is to acknowledge that if your territory consists of clients and prospects, the amount of potential revenue outside of your existing buyers usually dwarfs what is represented by the current contacts within your customer base. Good sales managers know that they must balance the time of their sales team between selling additional products to their customer base and selling additional solutions to other buyers.

These "other buyers" may be within existing customer accounts or may be brand-new accounts. Typically, sales quotas will reflect this opportunity and will mirror the company's year-over-year growth plans. This is because most technology companies spend a lot of time, effort and expense on securing the first product or solution within an account. You usually have many other products to sell once the prospect becomes your customer!

The theory here is that if you make the customer successful with the first product, you will have the inside track on additional opportunities. The prospect should favor the sales team and your solutions because he is already familiar with the quality of your solutions and support and (presumably) already enjoys working with your account team. Sometimes the additional products can be sold to the buyer of the first solution, and sometimes they will require going to other line-of-business executives within the account. Failure by the sales manager or any salesperson to go after all of these markets usually means falling short of the annual budget.

SANDLER TIP

If you make the customer successful with the first product, you will have the inside track on additional opportunities.

MOVING BEYOND THE COMFORT ZONE

If most sales managers and sales staff believe making the customer happy with the first product opens the door to further sales, why do we find so much prospecting reluctance within technology sales teams? Why are there so many excuses when it comes to prospecting?

Having managed technology sales teams for over 25 years, I believe that I have heard from both salespeople and their managers every possible reason, justification and/or excuse for avoiding prospecting, with the possible exception of, "My dog ate the prospect." I suspect that one's on the way.

Some of these excuses were pure baloney, and we both knew it. Others were "head trash" (a problem that lies between the ears) that the sales manager or salesperson had convinced themselves represented reality.

A great example of this second kind of excuse occurred when I was a VP at Cullinet Software. Cullinet was the market leader of its time and was the first software company to be listed on the New York Stock Exchange. It made a name for itself by providing a high-performance database for IBM mainframes. We had many experienced salespeople who had been successful selling our database products to database administrators and application development teams. Our second major product line was a suite of integrated financial and manufacturing applications, built with our development tools on top of our database. This suite required our sales teams to reach out to chief financial officers, logistics managers, manufacturing executives and other line-of-business managers with whom the sales teams had no contact or relationship. While many of our account executives were able to prospect effectively to these new buyers, we still had many successful salespeople who struggled with the requirement to reach out to new people. The salespeople who had the least difficulty calling on functional executives typically had done this kind of prospecting at some earlier point in their career. For them, this new approach was already within their comfort zone. Those who struggled the most tended to have a background of selling strictly to information technology managers within application development and database departments. For them, calling on VPs of manufacturing and CFOs was so far outside of their comfort zone that it often looked like they would need a plane ticket to get there.

Even when training was provided on how to approach these prospects, what to say when you got there and what the sales process should look like after the initial discussion, many of our sales professionals were neither willing nor able to execute in this new market. The most common excuse was, "Our current customer contact for our database product has told me not to reach out to any of these functional buyers." Now, our clients were Fortune 500 manufacturing companies. One day I mapped out on a whiteboard for the latest account executive who gave me this excuse at least 50 other software companies with similar solutions to ours who were in the process of calling on our customer, without getting permission from our database contact. We then made a call on the customer to explain this to him and gain his concurrence that, since there was no way to prevent this kind of discussion from happening with other vendors, didn't it make sense for him to participate with us in this discussion? He agreed, but I expected that much. This was just another reason concocted within the salesperson's head (more of that "head trash") to justify prospecting reluctance.

In this case, I suspect the person believed the reason he gave to be a valid one. In other cases, the salesperson knows full well that the excuse is bogus. Either way, these are problems that exist only in the mind. These problems must be effectively addressed in order to resolve someone's prospecting reluctance.

> ### SANDLER TIP
>
> *The single most common reason head trash occurs in salespeople is the salesperson's failure to separate his identity as a person from the role he plays as a prospecting salesperson.*

WHY HEAD TRASH HAPPENS

Prospecting reluctance takes many shapes. For some salespeople, it takes the form of a lack of cold calls; for others, a failure to ask for introductions or referrals; for others, an unwillingness to sell new products to new buyers, even within an existing customer organization. All of these are examples of the "what" of prospecting reluctance, though. What's far more important is the "why." The single most common reason head trash occurs in salespeople is the salesperson's failure to separate his identity as a person from the role he plays as a prospecting salesperson.

Salespeople who fuse their identity and their role take all rejections personally, including such events as unreturned phone calls, an unwillingness to meet and the inevitable, "No thanks, we're fine," responses. As a result, they stay within their existing comfort zone by, as an example, calling on people they already know to discuss products they already know. Even though this kind of call may not lead to the achievement of their budget goals, it does lead to their maintaining their comfort zone goals. Conversely, getting to people they don't know to discuss other products with which they may not be that familiar could lead to overachieving their budget goals. But in their minds, this kind of call will lead to them not maintaining their comfort zone goals. So they avoid it.

SANDLER TIP

There's a famous Sandler Rule that goes as follows: "You don't have to like prospecting. You just have to do it."

REMOVING THE HEAD TRASH

At Sandler, we address this problem by helping salespeople view their role as a prospector as one of many roles they play in life. Most salespeople are also spouses, children, friends, coworkers, neighbors, coaches and so on and could honestly be rated nines or tens (on a scale of one to ten) in each of these roles. Given these facts, how can the response of a stranger who knows neither you nor your solution (for example, someone who hangs up on a cold call) possibly be taken as a personal insult?

When prospecting is viewed as a role rather than as part of who you are (your identity), it becomes more of a game and less of a life-altering experience. The sales manager is then able to focus on ensuring that the salesperson follows the behaviors required to be successful. A prospecting "cookbook" is created. This lists all of the activities identified as best practices for the sales role. For instance: on a weekly/monthly basis, how many prospecting calls, introduction requests, meetings with new department heads within existing customers and so on do the sales manager and the salesperson agree can be completed?

The focus then is clear. Working together, the salesperson and the manager ensure that the activities in the cookbook occur on time. By working with Sandler, our clients have proven time after time that if you do the right activities at the right level of frequency, you will get the right results. There's a famous Sandler Rule that goes as follows: "You don't have to like prospecting. You just have to do it."

It takes less time than you may think to learn to follow that rule. When salespeople actually start to see the results from these efforts, they begin to calculate the commission dollars that are sure to follow. Once that happens, they are well on their way to overcoming their prospecting reluctance. That's the point at which they understand that they don't need to like prospecting—they just need to do it!

KEY TAKEAWAYS

- When prospecting is viewed as a role, rather than as part of who you are (your identity), it becomes more of a game and less of a life-altering experience.
- Schedule your prospecting time in stone and work all of your other activities around these times.
- No new customers are going to drive up to your desk. You have to find them.

CHAPTER 6

The Stress-Free Sales Call

A successful prospecting salesperson must believe the following statement to be 100 percent true: In the first two minutes of a cold call, the salesperson no more knows that the prospect needs to buy his solution than the prospect knows that he does not need the solution. So your, "You would be crazy not to buy from me," is as equally ludicrous as their telling you, "We don't know what you're selling but we don't need it!" Prospects get calls all day long from salespeople who start slinging features and benefits as soon as the prospect says "hello." If you change your mindset from, "Pick up the phone and I will sell you," to, "Pick up the phone and let's see if we should even be speaking," you'll be surprised when they don't answer your initial questions as opposed to being surprised when they do.

SANDLER TIP

In the first two minutes of the cold call, the salesperson no more knows that the prospect needs to buy than the prospect knows that he does not need the solution.

At Sandler we have a saying: "Your outlook dictates your results." Let's look at what that means in practical terms, as it relates to a prospecting phone call made to someone in the high-tech space. If a salesperson believes that a prospect would not want to speak with him, his approach on the phone usually leads to a result that will reinforce that belief. Maybe this has happened to you. You may have suffered from the "three too's" of prospecting: too much talking, selling too soon and sounding too "salesy."

These mistakes stem from you being outside of your comfort zone when you make the call. They manifest themselves in both the words and the tone you employ. Have you ever heard of the "fight or flight" response—the defense mechanism woven deeply into the human nervous system? When you initiate a dangerous or uncertain situation by sounding like every other nervous salesperson who cold-calls a prospect, a response of "flight" is triggered in the prospect's mind. The prospect starts looking for the quickest way to dismiss this unwanted interruption.

It's a vicious cycle. You're uncomfortable and nervous, which puts you into a mode where both your tone and your words doom you to failure. This failure then reinforces the lack of comfort on your very next call, and so on. (By the way, the reason I'm so certain about the existence of the vicious cycle is that I experienced it myself at the beginning of my career!)

The correct approach would be to sound different in a good way, with a tone that is engaging without being too pushy. The goal is to quickly get the prospect talking, with the salesperson saying as few words as possible. We call this the "stress-free sales call." It is designed to remove any pressure in the conversation for both the salesperson and the prospect.

People often ask me whether this call is scripted or not. The answer is that this call is a hybrid model where the first 90 seconds are usually scripted and the rest is unscripted. But the total call lasts as long as ten minutes when things are going well—a length that is pretty much unheard of in any scripted "cold" prospecting call.

SANDLER TIP

The best calling approach for prospecting is a hybrid model where the first 90 seconds or so of the call is mapped out ahead of time, and the balance is unscripted.

Let's take a look at what needs to be addressed when cold-calling prospects.

THE PATTERN INTERRUPT

The first thing that must be addressed is the prospect's initial reflex response to cold-calling salespeople. We overcome this by using the principle of human curiosity. There are countless variations, but it could sound something like this:

> Hi, Bill, this is Rich from So-and-So company. I'm not even sure if we need to have a conversation today. Would it be OK if I briefly explain what I do, and then you decide whether we continue the conversation?

Most respondents will respond positively to this approach. If the prospect ever says that you have called at a bad time, just ask when would be a better time to call back. Chances are that there isn't a better time, so right now is just as good (or bad) as any other time!

Remember, the goal here is not only to get you into a comfort zone for making these calls, but also to make the prospect comfortable with participating. Most people resent taking cold calls because they don't know how long they will last, don't know where the salesperson is going and do not look forward to being pushed around. Isn't that what you feel like prior to making the decision to end an incoming prospecting call?

Our approach lets prospects feel as though they are in control of the call at all times. When you pose a question like the above, both your words and your tone should indicate that you are not sure that the person is even the right person for you to talk to within the account. The reason for this will become clear in a moment.

THE 30-SECOND COMMERCIAL

If you've done your job correctly, the prospect up to this point has been engaged in helping you understand whether he is the correct contact. This is the unstated or stated question of the early portion of the call, and it opens the door for the salesperson to use a well-crafted 30-second commercial.

This commercial is similar to the example that we created for the iPhone. Using the technique we illustrated in the earlier chapter on value propositions, it might sound like this:

> I am John Smith with ABC Corporation. Customers like you work with us because they are frustrated over the high cost of X, challenged by the complexities of the current government regulations with regard to Y, or concerned about their ability to increase their profits while dealing with the impact of Z. I don't know, are any of these a concern for you, Bill?

Notice what we did here. We took the three biggest problems that the solution solves and incorporated them into that 30-second commercial. We prefaced each one of those problems with a pain word (i.e., frustrated, challenged, concerned) to help trigger a response if indeed the prospect is currently dealing with one of these issues. In essence we defined the solution not by its features, but by the problems it solves. We used this approach to both engage the prospect now and subsequently qualify him for further conversations. By the way, it only works if once you pose the question, you actually stop talking. That question may lead to a silence. Your job is to step back, keep your mouth shut and let the person on the other end of the line respond.

If the prospect identifies with one or more of these pain points, you would use a softening statement such as, "You are not alone," or, "Seems like everyone I'm talking to these days has the same issues." This positive reinforcement keeps the prospect comfortable and encourages additional participation. You would then go right into an Up-Front Contract.

THE UP-FRONT CONTRACT

Notice that the up-front contract used on this call is not an attempt to get the prospect to agree to buy anything. It might sound like this:

> Bill, I am not sure if I can solve your problem yet, but may I make a suggestion? How about if we take a few minutes and you allow me to ask you a few questions? Are you OK with that?

If you've done your job properly, Bill will say "yes." You would then complete your up-front contract along these lines:

> Great. That way, at the end of our conversation we should have arrived at either one of two possibilities. Either one

of us may decide that we are not a good fit. If you feel that way, can I count on you to tell me so?"

[Get agreement.]

On the other hand, we might both decide that the issue merits a follow-up call. If so, will you tell me that as well?

[Again, gain the agreement.]

Perfect. Because, since we are only going to decide on whether we should have a next call, can we agree that neither of us should have to say "let me think it over" at the end, since that would mean that we did not use this time wisely?

[Final agreement, and maybe a knowing chuckle.]

Thanks, Bill.

Just as you did in the early part of the conversation, the up-front contract makes the prospect feel in control. First, you're asking ahead of time for various permissions. Second, you're being absolutely up front. you're letting the prospect know exactly what you're doing, and you're being very clear. Remember, you're only deciding on another conversation, not trying to close a sale on this call. If you do this right and approach the person respectfully, the person you're calling will have a vested interest in qualifying in or out for further conversations.

All of this typically takes less than 90 seconds.

FISHING FOR PAIN

What you've just read ends the scripted portion of the stress-free sales call. From this point on, the Sandler-trained sales professional uses questioning strategies and techniques to take the prospect through the Sandler Pain Funnel® (about which I'll share more later) in an attempt to qualify or disqualify the prospect from further sales activities. At this point, you're fishing for pain.

> So let's get started, Bill. You mentioned that all three of these topics are a concern. Which would you say is the highest priority? Tell me more about that. Where are you today, and where would you like to be?

Although you can and should have your first "big" question prepared ahead of time, the prospect should do most of the talking from this point forward in the call. Your job is to play off the prospect's statements and responses.

Experience with hundreds of thousands of salespeople has proven that if you follow this calling approach and if the prospect really is suffering with these business pains, he will have no problem sharing them with you—even during an unscheduled cold call. In the worst-case scenario, the prospect may ask you to call back when more time is available. This is why there is no need to request more than a few minutes.

Think about it. If the prospect has no pain, the call will be over quickly. That's good for both of you. On the other hand, if prospects have one or more of these pains, they will give you more than a few minutes. So why scare them off by asking for 15 or 20 minutes up front?

CLOSE FOR THE APPOINTMENT

Once you believe that both the company and this person are prospects, you would then suggest setting up another call or visit using an up-front contract. That might sound like this:

Based upon what you have told me, it would seem to make sense for you, me and the other interested parties, Mike and Jane, to set up a conference call to dig a little deeper into these issues. We will need for you to schedule about an hour of their time. Are you OK doing this?

[Get the *yes.*]

Great. The objective of this next call will be for both sides to exchange enough information on issues and possible solutions to see if it makes sense for our companies to fully engage in resolving the problems. Now, if at any time during the call any of us uncover something that indicates that we are not a fit, we need to let the rest of us know this has occurred. Can we count on your team letting us know if this occurs? Also, if it looks like we might be a fit for you, we will work out an action plan at the end of our next call. Will your team be OK with that as well?

[Again, get the *yes*.]

Perfect. We do not want to end the call unaware of whether we should or should not be exploring this further. Agreed?

[Get agreement.]

Thanks, Bill. Oh, one more thing. Can you and the team give some thought prior to the next call as to what you would need in any alternative solution that would make your company want to take action? Thanks, Bill, talk to you soon.

> ### SANDLER TIP
> *Our goal is to obtain information during the qualifying call, not provide it!*

POST-SELL THE APPOINTMENT

Because the pains that prospects discuss may not last forever, you want to post-sell the next appointment to decrease the likelihood of it being postponed or canceled. That post-sell might sound like this:

You know Bill, sometimes when I speak with people such as yourself, I find that they want this next step to occur, but then after we hang up other priorities pop up and sometimes these meetings get postponed or canceled. Can you see that happening here?

The typical response from Bill, your prospect, would feature words to the effect that he can see how that could occur but he won't let that happen here. That's what you want to hear.

I want you to notice what happened here. You've taken out your biggest concern and fear and put it right on the table. You may even "milk it" a little bit, presenting yourselves as struggling with the problem a little more deeply than just depicted. The result is, in most cases, a "rescue" response from the prospect ("I won't let that happen here"), which will make it that much harder for the prospect not to deliver on the commitments for the next meeting.

IT WORKS—IN HIGH-TECH AND EVERYWHERE ELSE

By using this approach, you are far more likely to get a conversation started with the prospect than if you simply recite a feature-heavy script from the beginning of the conversation to the end, which is what our competition does and what the prospect expects.

One of the biggest challenges for the salesperson in the tech space (or any space) is learning how to hold back on the product knowledge. The whole point of the prospecting call is to avoid starting to sell when you should be qualifying by letting the prospect do the talking. Remember: Your goal is to obtain information during the qualifying call, not provide it!

KEY TAKEAWAYS

- Experience with hundreds of thousands of salespeople has proven that if you follow the calling approach in this chapter and if the prospect really is suffering with business pains that are relevant to what you do, he will have no problem sharing them with you, even during an unscheduled cold call.
- By using the concept of "struggling" in your opening, you make the prospect feel OK about himself.
- Most people who struggle with a business problem cannot resist speaking about it, even to a stranger.

CHAPTER 7

Diagnosis or Treatment?

W hen my family and I moved to New York to run sales for Computer Associates (CA), the first thing my wife and I looked for was a local doctor who was respected within the community.

I got a recommendation from some of the other CA executives for a certain physician—I'll call him Dr. Jones. I asked why they were so positive about this particular individual. My CEO said, "There are hundreds of doctors who can treat you correctly once you are properly diagnosed. But for every hundred of those doctors, there may be just one who always gets the diagnosis correct. This guy gets the diagnosis right."

Translation: Nobody wants to be treated for the wrong illness!

That thought has stayed in my mind for the past two decades.

(And, that physician has remained our family doctor the whole time.) I mention this story because it's deeply relevant to success in the world of sales. What separates the great trusted advisors— the true sales professionals—from everybody else? They're better diagnosticians! That's true of successful salespeople in general, and it is certainly true of successful salespeople who sell technology solutions.

> ### SANDLER TIP
>
> *If you treat the patient before you diagnose the problem, that's malpractice.*

The ability to diagnose before attempting to "treat the patient" separates the masters from everyone else. You know what? There are not all that many master diagnosticians working as professional salespeople in the high-tech space.

Perhaps you're wondering why that is. Here's my explanation. Most salespeople aren't comfortable with the pain interrogation process that is a natural part of sales. In fact, many view it as a mental checkmark, something that should be completed as quickly as possible. If, by some chance, they happen to bring out the personal pains and needs of the prospect, they become uncomfortable seeing the prospect squirm while talking about current business problems and their associated frustrations. When you combine prospects being outside of their comfort zones (because they're starting to reveal their real needs) and salespeople being outside of their comfort zones (because they're less comfortable with diagnosing than they are with feature selling), the result is usually a predictable one. There is a rush to wrap up the diagnosis (the pain identification) and start talking about the treatment (selling).

SANDLER TIP

Nobody wants to be treated for the wrong illness!

(MIS)DIAGNOSIS

Many people, especially those who lead with the "D" communication style from DISC, use this "hurry up and treat me" approach when they visit the doctor. Don't ask me why, but they do.

To hear them talk, you would think they'd prefer treatment to begin in the elevator, while they're on the way up to the doctor's office. That's how I used to be, before I was lucky enough to find my present doctor. For years, I was one of the patients that good physicians learn to accommodate. Often while the doctor was examining me, I would explain what I felt was wrong with me in order to speed up the process. I would even suggest to him what I thought was the medical problem.

What causes patients like me to do this kind of thing? That's an answer worth exploring, since salespeople, like doctors, run into their fair share of patients like me. It could be anything from our "I'm in a hurry" personalities, to our anxiety about losing control of the process (whether in a hospital or a conference room). We could be nervous about what we might find out as a result of the discussion, or it could be simple force of habit because this is how we're used to dealing with people. All I can tell you is, it took me a while to give it up. It could just be that, for most of us patients, discussing our health in a doctor's office puts us outside of our comfort zone.

SANDLER TIP

The salesperson is doing the right thing by getting the prospect who may not know the salesperson all that well to take the time to explore what the real issues are.

A doctor who is trying to do the right thing by tactfully resuming control of the conversation from a "D" patient is no different from a salesperson also trying to do the right thing. The salesperson is doing the right thing by getting a prospect who may not know the salesperson all that well to take the time to explore what the real issues are. Helping defuse any business-problem anxiety over what may emerge as the real issue is the right thing.

The great physicians take all the vital signs, do all the blood work, run the necessary X-rays, check the family history and so on—all to avoid treating the wrong problem. They know the symptoms of the patient could be identical (at first glance) to the symptoms of a whole lot of different illnesses. In the same way, great salespeople avoid rushing through the diagnosis to begin treatment as soon as possible. They want to avoid (mis)treating business symptoms that could come from many different root causes.

SYMPTOM OR PROBLEM?

Let's take a look at how this applies to the world of sales training. When I am approached by a CEO or a vice president of sales about a possible engagement, it is rarely because the sales engine is going like gangbusters and the whole company, including all of the executive team members, is overjoyed with the results of the current business development process. Yet I know that sales volume not being where it needs to be is a symptom—not a problem!

Just as a doctor must understand the true significance of a fever, a swollen joint or a headache, I need to understand the root cause of the undesirable sales volume before attempting to treat anything. Now, I've never gone to medical school. But I do know enough to follow a proven diagnostic process before I try to fix anything.

At Sandler, we utilize many assessment tools that connect to things like sales skills, sales process, value proposition and even customer satisfaction, which we can measure with interviews. We assess all of these things so we can ascertain the root cause of the symptoms the prospect presents. While we hope that the root cause is something we can address, that is not always the case. If the prospect has a product or service that is overpriced and under-functioning for its target audience, we can prescribe all the sales training medicine in the world and probably not get the desired result. On the other hand, if the product and pricing are still competitive and the issue is one requiring a different sales process, skills or behaviors, sales training might be the best medicine. Even in this situation, our conversations and diagnostic activities must continue to ensure we get to the real problem. Prospects hardly ever bring us the real issue the first time.

There are several reasons this occurs. It could be that the prospect himself is unsure what the root cause is because he is an integral part of the problem. There is an old Sicilian saying that can be translated as: "The hunchback cannot see the hump on his own back." Fortunately, most of the people in our market are reasonably intelligent. If they knew what they were doing to diminish their expected results, they wouldn't continue to do it. They just need to talk to the right diagnostician. One of the great values of having a trusted advisor like a Sandler trainer for a CEO or business unit executive is that the outsider has both the skills and the fortitude to ask the tough questions and help executives think through the problem in a way they probably never have before.

Another common reason prospects rarely bring us the real issue in the first meeting has to do with their own comfort level in discussing important issues with a relative stranger. Most prospects can overcome this issue if the salesperson creates a dialogue centered on diagnosing the problem rather than selling the solution. Using sales training as an example, I might engage the client as follows:

You know, when people tell me that sales aren't where they need to be, I always ask them if they feel the biggest short-fall is in the acquisition of new customers or in the growth of revenue from existing accounts. Which do you feel it is within your company?

Sometimes prospects will say "both," but usually we start a process of honest dialogue around whether the biggest problem is that they're not adding enough new accounts because the salespeople won't prospect or they're not doing a good enough job of making current customers successful in order to sell them additional products.

The distinction is an important one. A sales initiative centered on finding new accounts would have an entirely different set of necessary behaviors than one centered on growing existing accounts.

Here's an example of what that same kind of early conversation with a prospect might sound like. Let's say that you are selling CRM to a prospect. The prospect initially tells you that the problem with the current solution is that the salespeople are not entering the information. The salespeople complain that the current solution is too difficult to use and takes away from their selling time. The symptom here is that the salespeople are not using the CRM system. Further investigation is needed by the CRM salesperson to ascertain the root cause of this problem, which could be: the user interface; the lack of training; they are being asked to enter too much data; no one has built a "win" for the salespeople to use the system; the salespeople view any CRM as another way for management to spy on them; etc. Since the prospect executive probably does not know the real answer here, your ability to help diagnose the problem and then show how your CRM solution could address the root cause of the issue will make you stand out among the other CRM peddlers as a trusted advisor.

I hope you can see the value of making sure you are actually treating the problem, not a symptom. Sales "peddlers" start selling too soon. They think selling means hacking away at symptoms. They never gain deep insights, and they never win trusted-advisor status.

Good sales managers have learned through trial and error that a proper business-problem diagnosis will greatly improve and expedite the prospect qualification process. This process tells both the manager and the salesperson:

- How big a problem this is. (The bigger the problem, the easier it is to garner executive support for budget dollars and action plans later on.)
- Whether proposed solutions will deliver the desired result. (You want to be a square peg in a square hole.)

Some salespeople make the mistake of believing it is an act of determination to never disqualify prospect. They see even the vaguest expression of interest, even the tiniest glimmer of a fit with their solution, as a sign from above. They begin the process of trying to put a square peg in a round hole in order to solve a small, or even nonexistent, problem.

Superior salespeople cultivate a sense of abundance and avoid this behavior. They recognize that their own time is a dwindling resource. They want to avoid the "square peg in a round hole" scenario and have no desire to start a fruitless sales process. They know that there are many, many more qualified prospects still out there to find and engage!

KEY TAKEAWAYS

- Sales "peddlers" start selling too soon. They think selling means hacking away at symptoms. They never gain deep insights, and they never win trusted-advisor status. Superior salespeople cultivate a sense of abundance and avoid this behavior.
- Prospects rarely bring you the real problem first.
- Your ability to help the prospect accurately diagnose and then cure the real business ailment will make you, the salesperson, the biggest part of your solution's value proposition.

CHAPTER 8

Pain Is the Best Impending Event!

Y ou don't need a long tenure of selling within the high-tech industry to experience the agony of having your deals evaporate after they've been committed to your forecast.

Everyone who sells for a living in this industry has experienced this angst. The question is, why is it so common? In part, it's because technological solutions are fundamentally conceptual in their value. They usually replace either a manual or an ineffective automated solution, and that means the customer always has a fallback scenario. Unlike people selling some of the other means of production such as raw materials, shipping services or additional factory space, salespeople selling a new technical solution face a special challenge. Unless they have uncovered an extremely pressing need with a strong return on investment

(ROI) connected to the corresponding solution, many sales-people and therefore many sales managers find themselves in the position where they need the deal to happen far more than the prospect needs to buy the solution. That's not a great place to be from either a negotiating or closing-the-deal position.

SANDLER TIP

Unless you have uncovered an extremely pressing need with a strong return on investment that's connected to your solution, you will find yourself in the position where you need the deal to happen far more than the prospect needs to buy the solution.

If you'd like to test how vulnerable your current forecast is to this problem, ask yourself that same question from Chapter Two: "If I stopped calling all the prospects in my pipeline, how long would it be before any of them picked up the phone and called me?" That question, of course, leads to the next question: "How many of my prospects would never call me?"

A SOLUTION TO THE PROBLEM

Very early in my sales career I had the good fortune of working for IBM. They understood that the problem of deal evaporation would occur and that it stood in the way of the sales organization providing an accurate forecast that the management team needed to run the company effectively. IBM, accordingly, placed extremely heavy emphasis on the need to find a big problem within a big account in order to extract big dollars.

> ### SANDLER TIP
> *You must find a big problem within a big account in order to extract big dollars.*

Management at IBM also recognized something else: the simple fact that a company might need what you are selling doesn't mean that it will spend the money at the levels you anticipate or according to your schedule. A very different corporate need or an even more pressing problem for this prospect might supersede the need for your solution and either temporarily or permanently postpone your sale.

What IBM taught me back then has stayed with me over decades and still rings true for me today. You are always at risk with your forecast if the deal is viewed only by the sales team as "our deal" instead of being viewed that way by the prospect as well.

Thus, your objective should always be to find and qualify a prospect and subsequently build a business justification based on the proposition that the prospect needs to obtain and implement your solution at least as much as you need to sell it—perhaps even more. This situation is not as rare as most salespeople imagine. It is almost always tied to finding an impending event for the prospect that has significant ramifications if the prospect does not address that event. If you don't have that kind of situation, don't forecast the sale!

DO THEY WANT YOUR SOLUTION AS MUCH AS YOU WANT THE SALE?

Let me use my own experience at IBM as an example. We knew our forecast was solid when the prospect showed us a cancellation letter to the manufacturer of the computer system we would be replacing. The prior system was a capital asset of our competitor. Once the competitor knew that his product would be coming off maintenance, he notified the customer (our prospect) that he had already found another home for this computer asset and he would be picking up the system on a certain date without any opportunity to extend its lease. This typically meant that the only way we would miss our forecast for the revenue from our computer would be if we somehow dropped the ball in the sales or installation process.

We would set up a parallel processing period when both machines would be present and both the prospect and IBM knew the date that the prior manufacturer's computer would be unplugged. Unless our prospect planned on running the company without any computer for some period of time (not likely!), the forecasted date was always solid.

Many of the salespeople we train at Sandler believe that their prospects do not or cannot present them with this kind of unmovable impending event. We always say in response: "Impending events can be created in qualified prospects, as long as you focus on the personal pain of the buyer."

Too often, salespeople and their management offer major buying incentives early in the sales cycle, using tools such as discounts, which bear little or no resemblance to the scenario described above.

It all comes down to pain. I commonly run into three different kinds of pain: surface, business and personal. For many salespeople, the instinct is to cut short the hard work of questioning, qualifying and uncovering the real business and personal need by attempting to close as soon as they hear a whisper about some form of surface-level pain. The most common tactic is to provide prospects with a price quote containing a discount that is only valid through their forecast (this week, month or quarter, as the case may be). The salesperson subsequently sees this price and the associated discount as a strong enough impending event to ensure that the deal occurs on the correct time schedule. It almost never does.

For one thing, prospects have heard this before from many other salespeople. They know they're being manipulated, and that lowers the trust in the relationship. For another thing, they know darn well that if they come to you after the deadline and tell you that they decided to go with your competitor because you are now raising the price, you will not only offer them the prior discount but will most likely cut the price even deeper to win the deal. This, by the way, is the textbook example of the salesperson who needs a deal to happen far more than the prospect.

The problem is, this is the only "impending event" that many salespeople know how to generate. This creates a behavioral change in prospects, who will now time all of their purchases to occur at the end of the quarter for all of their vendors. In the high-tech industry this is called the "hockey stick" effect since it leads to sales-quarter charts that are flat in months one and two with a big increase (thus the image of a hockey stick) in the third month.

Think about the deals you were fortunate enough to experience in which the prospect was driving the process forward. If you've been selling for more than a year, you've probably experienced this situation. My guess is that if you're like me, you found that very few of these impending events were tied to some magical discount. Most or all of them were tied to a business or personal pain that needed to be addressed.

MOVING BEYOND THE DISCOUNT

To create this form of "buyer passion" in a prospect, top salespeople understand that they need to qualify both the company and the buyer.

Most salespeople think a qualified prospect is "someone who will talk to me." Actually, people who are qualified have a problem you can solve, a budget with which you can work and a decision process they are willing to share with you.

One of David Sandler's great discoveries was that people buy for emotional reasons and then later back up their decision with facts. This point bears very close study. It is not enough to uncover that a company needs your solution unless you also uncover the person within the account who has the biggest personal gain to achieve by alleviating the business problem your solution solves.

Typical buying emotions stem from the child ego-state made famous in the psychological theory known as "transactional analysis." Some technical solutions, such as security, disaster recovery and data loss, lend themselves to the emotion of fear. You might not think a child is leading the way in such a situation, but that's what's happening.

In much the same way that people buy insurance because of a fear of what might happen if they don't have it, sometimes the fear of pain that could occur in the future motivates the buyer to take action to secure specific technology solutions.

Many more technical solutions lend themselves to be the alleviation of an existing problem. Most people will react to resolving an existing problem even before addressing a future pain. By the same token, sometimes fear of a future event becomes an existing problem. For example, when a company suffers a security breach, loss of data or failed attempt at utilizing the disaster recovery plan, the present problem is right there and points to a potential future pain, perhaps even bigger.

That is why it's so important during the qualification stage that you identify the pain and thereby the motivation that will cause prospective tech buyers to take action. Never bridge the gap from qualifying into selling (i.e., fulfillment) until you have uncovered rock-solid reasons for the prospect to move forward with you as a peer in your sales process.

When you arrive at that point in the qualification process,

you should ask the prospect about this directly. What you ask should sound like this: "Is X something you would like to explore solving with us?" Once the prospect says "yes," you have just been empowered to create a mutual action plan (MAP). The prospect has agreed that he would like to explore your solution to see if it gets him out of this business and personal pain state. The key here is to remember that you, the salesperson, are still in the qualification stage. You haven't entered fulfillment!

What you say next to launch the action plan process might sound something like this:

> May I make a suggestion? Can we create a list of activities that both you and I would have to accomplish to take us from where we are now to either a *yes* or *no* decision on our solution? I'm not asking you to guarantee that you are going to buy from us. Rather, I am asking that you agree to an open and frank process of getting to one of those two decision points. Do you agree this would be a good use of our time?

If you've done a good job of qualifying up to this point, more times than not the prospect should agree to what you propose. Your suggestion makes logical sense and is predicated on the idea that neither you nor the prospect is going to have to waste any time or effort.

In the MAP, both the prospect and the salesperson should have to-do tasks with deadlines assigned to them. Your activities might include additional discovery calls, presentations, demonstrations and perhaps even a proof of concept. Don't let the word "presentation" fool you. None of that counts as fulfillment! You're qualifying with increasing detail and accuracy. The prospect's action items might include verifying budget, inviting other stakeholders to your events, getting the company's legal people to look at your agreement and securing additional exposure within the company for both you and your sales management. You are qualifying the prospect for the decision process. The deal has now gone from being "your deal" to being "our deal."

SANDLER TIP

In the mutual action plan, both the prospect and the salesperson should have to-do tasks with deadlines assigned to them.

What happens to the prospect who doesn't want to create a MAP and wants you to do whatever he asks, in perpetuity? What do you think? If you're smart, you'll close the file and move on to another opportunity. This person typically doesn't represent the same likelihood of closing as someone who does agree to a MAP. He most certainly does not represent a deal that can be forecasted with any degree of confidence. When you run into "prospects" like these, ask yourself, "Why do they need to buy from me—and why now?" If you cannot answer those questions and they cannot provide good answers, move on to the next one.

Personal pain is the best impending event. It trumps motivational discounts given to prospects whose timelines and personal needs remain a mystery to you. When I was senior VP of sales at an integration software company, we qualified our bigger prospects by getting them to pay for production data trials. We did this for one simple reason. We knew that once the business unit executive saw that an existing business problem the company had could be solved with our solution, there would be little chance that the purchasing department would be allowed to let the trial expire. You see, the prospect had agreed that we would remove the software at the end of the trial period if he did not sign a license agreement. That's how we created a real impending event that provided us with negotiating leverage—and a deadline that was not based upon a bogus discount expiration.

KEY TAKEAWAYS

- You are always at risk with your forecast if the deal you are forecasting is viewed by the prospect as "your deal" instead of "our deal."
- Using a MAP creates a structured buying process that puts the salesperson at peer level with the prospect.
- Prospects should need to buy your solution at least as much as you need to make the sale.

CHAPTER 9

Selling to the Stakeholders

D avid Sandler once said that selling is like directing a Broadway show. Nowhere is that more true than in the high-tech space.

There are many similarities: lots of moving pieces; the need to find financing (i.e., business justification); the various stages of bringing the show to opening night (i.e., the sales cycle); and who knows, maybe even a few complex superstar personalities to deal with along the way. As with any major theatrical production, success depends on the director's ability to handle the various desires, fears, anxieties and egos of an interesting cast of characters in order for there to be a successful opening. The one big difference, though, is that, unlike a director, the salesperson usually doesn't get to choose the cast of characters.

The ensemble you work with is generally chosen for you. It is referred to collectively as the "stakeholders." Managing all the various requirements of all the stakeholders is a team undertaking. Typically, the account team that does the best job of handling these stakeholders wins the business.

HOW MANY STAKEHOLDERS?

Every major technology sale has four types of decisions that need to be made. These are 1) technical, 2) business, 3) financial and 4) political. The number of stakeholders involved in making these four decisions usually increases with both the size of the deal and the perceived resulting impact (either good or bad) on the prospect's business. The number of stakeholders also usually mirrors the culture of the prospect's business.

SANDLER TIP

The number of stakeholders involved in making decisions about your sale generally increases in proportion to the size of the deal and the perceived resulting impact (good or bad) upon the prospect's business.

Highly decentralized corporations that hold their business-unit leaders fully accountable for the profit and loss of their departments usually allow for more acquisition decisions to occur at the business-unit level. On the other hand, a highly centralized, top-down organization that has created a culture within its business units of utilizing common technology standards—i.e., one enterprise resource planning system, one common infrastructure for both security and storage, and so on—is more likely to control or influence the selection of any new technology, anywhere in the enterprise, from a corporate point of preference.

In the former situation, you will most likely have to sell to stakeholders within that one business unit. In the latter, you may have to identify and then sell to stakeholders both inside and outside of the business unit. It would not be uncommon for these outside-of-the-business-unit stakeholders to be located within a corporate infrastructure group that is some distance away from your initial contacts. In fact, they could be located on another continent!

Additionally, any stakeholder representing a corporate infrastructure group will most likely approach a proposal suggesting that he deviates from his corporate standards as an unnecessary evil, as something that should be prevented. This (common) state of affairs in the world of high-tech selling shows why the Sandler Selling System stresses that a prospect must be qualified not just for pain and budget, but also for the decision process as well.

This means finding out the *who, what, where, why, when* and *how* of the prospect's decision process and recognizing that the uncovered facts might just lead you to disqualify a prospect, even though he's qualified for both pain and budget. Some salespeople have a hard time getting their heads around this point, but it's an essential element of success in this space.

ARE THEY QUALIFIED FOR DECISION?

For example, if you knew that a company had already invested hundreds of millions of dollars in rolling out an ERP solution from a company based in Germany and that the corporate headquarters for that prospect's division was also based in Germany, you might not want to risk the time and effort required of an ERP sales cycle involving your own local U.S. division until the prospect can assure you that he has been given the authority to buy whatever vendor suits his business needs—even if the purchase means straying from the current corporate standard. Without gaining such an agreement, you run the risk of investing nine to twelve months in a sales cycle where you win the local decision but get stopped at corporate headquarters. That's no victory at all.

Unfortunately, you can't always take the prospect's word on this kind of thing. I wish I had a dollar for every technology sale that stalled after the local decision maker assured the salesperson that he had all the decision-making power, only to have the selection request get bounced because it deviated from a corporate standard. This is a lesson I've learned the hard way! I had a local CIO tell me once that when he questioned the corporate CIO as to why he was first told it was a local decision and was later overruled, the corporate CIO explained, "We were hoping that you would select what we are already using in the other divisions so that we would not have to over-rule your decision."

This is a painful lesson for any salesperson to learn, and it's particularly relevant to salespeople in the high-tech space. How do you avoid this problem? By identifying the full cast of characters, by verifying information from multiple sources and by being relentless in your pursuit of the identities, communication styles and subsequent pains of each stakeholder.

Below you'll see a chart of some of the typical decision-maker types we find in most high-tech sales.

NAME	TITLE	RESPONSIBILITY	DISC	FNE	STAKE/PAIN
Decision Maker					
User Buyer					
Tech Buyer					
Financial Buyer					
Key Influencers					

IDENTIFY THE CAST

During your initial qualification of the prospect, your goal is to identify which "characters" above will be in your Broadway play and "casting" the people who will play each part. Even if you are comfortable with the decision process as outlined by the prospect and you believe that it is a good investment of your time to move forward in the sales cycle, you still must identify all of these players.

Your job is to uncover not only each person's responsibility to the company (which is the real prospect, after all), but also the personal stake or pain that would motivate each individual to say "yes" or "no" to your proposed solution. Additionally, you need to determine after speaking with each stakeholder whether he is positive, negative or neutral towards making a change to your solution. Your goal, at a minimum, will be to get them all to a neutral or positive position since even one negative stakeholder can torpedo a deal.

Let's assume that you are selling a customer relationship management (CRM) system to a manufacturing company. Who might you find as the cast of characters filling these stakeholder roles?

In the hypothetical example, the decision maker is Bill, the president. He has the final say on budget dollars and the strategic direction of the company. The user buyer is the VP of sales, Francine, who has been pushing the president to make this investment. The technical buyer is an IT person named Jane, who needs to assess both the security of your cloud-based offering and its ability to scale to their future needs. The financial buyer is Mitch, a professional from the accounting office who will review your cost benefit analysis and provide the president with an unbiased opinion of the likelihood of achieving good returns on the investment. Your coach and chief ally within the account, also known as a "white knight," is Mel, the general manager of this business unit. Mel was your first point of contact. Mel is all about relationship-building, and he has been providing you with lots of guidance on how to get this business.

Every complex sale like this has key influencers—people who can't necessarily choose the vendor, but who can influence the decision in subtle but powerful ways. In this case, there are two. The first is Sam, who has built the current in-house system and has been working for the company for the past 15 years. Sam dislikes change. He knows that the company has outgrown his system, but he defines his own value to the company as being the owner and reigning expert on the current system. So, he is not in any real hurry to replace it.

The other key influencer is Mary, who used to work for this company as head of marketing and is highly respected by the president. Mary was so competent in her position that she was recruited to run both sales and marketing at another (noncompeting) company. Even though she is not technically on the org chart, President Bill will most likely seek her guidance at some point in the sales cycle.

ASSUME NOTHING!

One of the most common mistakes in enterprise sales comes when the salesperson assumes that the stakes and pains of the

final decision maker trickle down to each of the other stakeholders. In our example, if President Bill had a stated goal of increasing sales volume while lowering the company's cost of sales, it
would be very easy for you, the salesperson, to assume that the
other stakeholders share that same motivation. Assume nothing!

This problem is compounded when the decision makers are
assembled as a group for a presentation or demonstration. If you,
the salesperson, restate Bill's goal and ask whether any other issues should be included in the discussion, you may imagine that
by doing so, you are covering all the bases. You're not. Who in
their right mind is going to stand up in a forum with their peers
and superiors and tell Bill that your solution is additional work
for them personally or reveal a personal resentment about increasing their workload without increasing their compensation?

Get real. That person's secret hope is to find a way to torpedo
any new solution coming into the company. What's the best way
to accomplish this? By pretending to have an open mind.

What about Sam, who fears change in general and who views
your solution as a direct threat to his job security? Do you think
that Sam will bring this issue up in front of the other stakeholders?

GET MULTIPLE INFORMATION SOURCES

Clearly, Bill is not the only person about whom you need to
worry. You need to not only identify the stakeholders involved
in assessing your proposal, but to find a way to speak with each
member of the cast individually, even if only by phone.

This purpose of this is to take each person through an individual questioning sequence similar to what you accomplished with Mel, the business unit's general manager, when you qualified this opportunity. You must know the motivations and predispositions of everyone on the chart. There must be no gaps!

Using the correct communication styles and appropriate questioning techniques will enable you to complete your stakeholder chart. Let's tackle the communication styles piece of the equation first.

DISC

If you are not familiar with the DISC styles, here is a quick overview. In 1929, psychiatrist William Marston wrote that there are four distinct human behavioral patterns and therefore four distinct communication patterns:

1. Dominant (decisive, tough, impatient)
2. Influencer (sociable, talkative, open)
3. Steady Relator (calm, steady, laid back)
4. Compliant (precise, exact, analytical)

These patterns are distributed roughly equally across the human population. No pattern is more "right" than any other pattern. Since people prefer to be communicated with in one of these four styles, the salesperson who does not change his communication style to that of the one with whom he is speaking will only be properly communicating 25 percent of the time.

If this were Major League Baseball, you would get a multimillion dollar contract for a .250 batting average, or 25 percent. But this is high-tech sales. In this game, alienating 75 percent of the people with whom you communicate will usually get you sent back to the minors.

Making sense of all this is easier than you may think. Often, we can determine people's DISC style by the words they say or write in their emails. Test people's X-axis—their action vs. reserve orientation—first. Do they use words and phrases that are active and action-oriented, such as "sell," "do it," "win" and "succeed"? Or, do they use words and phrases that are more reserved and cautious, such as "plan," "process," "system" and "safeguard"?

On the Y-axis, check whether the words and phrases in the email lean toward the task at hand, as do words like "completion," "on time" and "must succeed." Or, do they include words and phrases that lean towards the people aspects of the task, as do "consensus," "morale," and "team approach"? Surprise! Once you have reliable samples of both data points, you can determine their DISC style (along with your own). See the chart below.

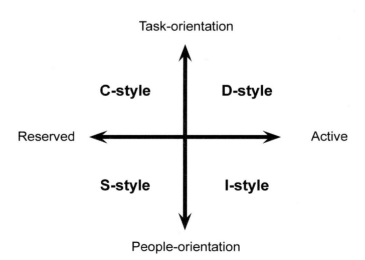

How you will communicate with each of these styles individually will vary greatly (see next chart).

How to communicate with a "D"	How to communicate with an "I"
• Be direct, brief, and to the point • Focus on the task, stick to business • Use a results-oriented approach • Identify opportunities/ challenges • Provide win/win situations • Use a logical approach • Touch on high points; do not overuse data • Do not touch; keep your distance	• Allow time for socialization • Lighten up; have fun • Ask for feelings and opinions • Use judicious touch (forearm and back) • Create a friendly, non-threatening environment • Involve the "I" and brainstorm new ideas and approaches • Expect quick decisions • Provide opportunities for recognition and reward
How to communicate with an "S"	How to communicate with a "C"
• Be patient • Draw out his/her opinions • Provide a logical approach to the facts • Relax; allow time for discussions • Show how solutions will benefit him/her • Clearly define all areas • Involve him/her in planning	• Use data and facts • Examine an argument from all sides • Keep on task; don't socialize • Disagree with the facts, not the person • Focus on quality • Avoid new solutions; stick to proven ideas • Do not touch • Allow time for him/her to think

Now let's return to the fictitious sales or marketing solution sale and identify some of the different DISC communication styles. President Bill is a net/net guy. He's not big on rapport or details, and he always wants to fast forward to the end of the story. He is a clear "D."

VP of Sales Francine is the user buyer. She is gregarious and friendly and always starts each conversation with small talk. Seems like you have an "I" there.

The technical buyer Jane has been in technology for over ten years. She has been certified in four different vendors' products and there never seems to be enough data for her to make a decision. Clearly her style is that of a "C."

The financial buyer Mitch is the analyst who has been assigned by the president and the CFO to challenge any ROI or payback calculation. Mitch is a spreadsheet jockey, a certified CPA who always uses words like "process" and "data." So there you have another "C" from a style viewpoint.

Your inside coach Mel is a combination. He is always friendly and loves to go to lunch and discuss family and sports, but he is also concerned about how the wrong decision could negatively affect his job. Seems like both an "I" and an "S." (Yes, you will occasionally run into people who combine two styles, but never three or four.)

Don't forget your friend Sam, who fears his own obsolescence and change. He is clearly an "S." You will need to get Sam alone and convince him that your solution has a role for him that will solidify his value to the company. You must make a commitment to him that you want him as a team member—and you must keep that commitment.

ONE ON ONE

Notice how each of these stakeholders may share some aspect of the same business level pain as President Bill but that they each will have different personal level pains and buying triggers that need to be identified and addressed.

First, you need to identify their current stance on your solution. The "FNE" column of the cast of characters chart is where you identify whether this person is a friend, neutral or enemy to your solution. This can only be ascertained through a one-on-one conversation. The best way to accomplish this is by getting to each person individually, prior to any group presentation or demo. That way you can use the Parent/Adult/ Child technique of transactional analysis to flush out and address all the individual issues. Here's what this might sound like with your friend Sam:

> Sam, if I were you, I might feel a little apprehensive about a new vendor and technology coming in and replacing both the people and the product that I had grown to know and trust over the years. I mean, we haven't even met, so if I were you, I would be questioning what role I would play if my company were to go with this solution. Is that a fair statement?
>
> [Sam agrees.]
>
> Look, let me assure you that I want you on our team. I can see what a great job you have done over the years with

the current vendor. I can only imagine what a valuable re-source you will be to both us and the business unit once we start working with you.

The point here is that you can't have that kind of conversation in a group. It is only in a one-on-one setting that you can probe for what each decision maker is trying to get out of this decision. You must probe for, and confirm, the most likely concern—even if it goes unstated by the prospect, as it often does.

OFF THE ORG CHART

Another thing to remember about stakeholders is that key in-fluencers may exist for your sales cycles outside of the org chart for the company to which you are selling. Remember Mary, the former head of marketing? Bill may not be her boss anymore, but he is not going to make this decision until he's convinced she thinks he's doing the right thing.

In my role as the EVP of global sales and Fortune 500 soft-ware companies, my quarterly duties included having some form of personal contact with the top 20 transactions we needed to make happen each quarter. Since this involved companies scat-tered around the globe and sales cycles that were 6–12 months long, I would sometimes visit the person the quarter before we thought a given deal had a realistic chance to close. By creating rapport with the decision maker, I avoided looking too trans-parent the following quarter when I either phoned or physically showed up to help get the transaction across the finish line.

Once, when I was doing this for the industry-leading CRM vendor, I came across a large transaction where we had supposedly been selected and approved by the financial people. But it was clear to me that the CIO was hesitant about pulling the contract trigger. When I probed for the reasons, the CIO informed me that the problem wasn't with me, but with him. (The last time I had heard that was in high school, when my girlfriend broke up with me.)

When I continued to probe, he leveled with me. He said that the last three major technical decisions his team had made had both major cost and time overruns. Neither he nor his peers had any real confidence in his team's ability to either select or deliver much more than the morning newspaper. Once my company had been "selected," he had contacted someone who used to work for him whose technical opinion he highly valued. When pressed with a "Should I go forward or not with what my team is recommending?" question, this trusted advisor honestly stated that he had no firsthand knowledge of either our company or our solution. As a result, everything had stopped cold.

It was clear to me that this person, who had been off my radar screen, did not want to make the CIO take action on something about which he had no knowledge. Instead he questioned why the CIO would take on any new projects at all. What was wrong with keeping the status quo in place?

I thanked the CIO for leveling with me, and our dialogue then focused on his (quite real) pain. This CIO was contemplating making no changes at all. We had identified the third-party with an opinion that he trusted, and we augmented our

proposal to include additional project management and professional services. The sales team then spent the next 60 days selling to this (hitherto unknown) trusted advisor of the CIO and
re-justifying the new proposal through the prospect company's
ROI process.

The good news is we closed a larger deal the following quarter. The bad news is that we could have gotten the same larger
deal a lot earlier had we done a better job in the initial Decision
Step of the Sandler selling process.

That story of mine is an important one for every salesperson in high-tech to consider. If you were the CIO of that company and your team had acquired several solutions that didn't
pan out, you too might not have full confidence in your team's
ability to make an accurate decision about a new solution. The
prospect wasn't bad for withholding information from me. I had
not done my job. I hadn't identified all the cast members, and I
didn't know what was most important to my main contact.

The big takeaway here is that not every influencer is on the
org chart. If you don't connect with every influencer, you not
only don't control the sale, but you are quite likely to lose it.
What would you say if a close friend of yours called and said:
"I'm thinking of switching vendors in a key strategic area for our
company—what do you think I should do?" Unless you have
firsthand knowledge of the current vendor and the proposed
new solution, you're going to be likely to say something like,
"Why switch?" You won't recommend a switch without knowing any of the facts.

Our sales cycle would have been better served by uncovering

this trusted advisor during the decision-qualification process, talking the project over with him one-on-one and inviting him to participate with the other stakeholders. We would have uncovered that this person's personal pain was the fear of giving the wrong advice to his friend, the CIO.

These days, I wait until all of the other stakeholders have been identified and then go to my main contact and say something like this:

I need to tell you something I'm struggling with. I know it may not be the case here, but often we go through decisions like this and at the very end a decision maker like you looks to friends and other business associates whose opinions they trust for additional advice. Can you identify someone like that that at the end of this process you might go to for some additional counsel?

[If yes:]

You know, you're not alone. Most people who make that type of decision do the same thing. May I make a suggestion? Rather than put you in the awkward position of trying to relay why you are making this decision and what our solution will bring to your company, we would be happy to include this person in all of our sales activities to the extent he [or she] is willing to participate. Even if the person only attends some of the sessions, that should make you more comfortable when you eventually do ask for his [or her] opinion. Is this something you would like us to do?

Invariably, the prospect agrees that any contact I have with this trusted advisor is going to greatly increase a positive outcome for everyone. Getting to all the stakeholders is the most critical part of selling to a qualified prospect in the high-tech market. Remember, there are three possible outcomes when it comes to making a decision (and only one of these pays): your solution, a competitor's solution, or no decision at all. It's that third outcome that salespeople who fail to get to all the stakeholders sometimes bring on themselves.

KEY TAKEAWAYS

- Expect multiple stakeholders and differing agendas. Each stakeholder will have different personal pains and buying triggers that need to be identified and addressed. You can only accomplish this by getting to each person individually, prior to any group presentation or demo.

- Look for external influencers for the decision who may not be on the organizational chart.

- Most "waste of time" sales cycles get started because the salesperson does not qualify the Decision Step with the same effort as the Pain and Budget Steps.

CHAPTER 10

All Prospects Are Not Created Equal

By now I hope it is crystal clear to you that most of your productivity as a salesperson (and therefore the bulk of your commissions) is tied to your ability to engage only qualified prospects. Yet you should also know that this part of the sales cycle—qualifying—has never been more difficult than today in the world of high-tech sales.

There have never been more salespeople trying to reach a single prospect. There have never been so many unqualified prospects using the Internet to research vendors prior to reaching out to a select few to request presentations and demonstrations. And selling time has never been so precious. Not even Sandler training can provide a 25th hour in the day! Take it all together, and what does it mean? As difficult as qualifying is today, it has never been more important. It is up to you to understand the definition of an "ideal prospect" and to create a disciplined approach by which prospects vie for your time.

SANDLER TIP

A sense of abundance should apply to both your prospecting and your sales efforts.

You've probably heard the saying, "Never go food shopping on an empty stomach." It's good advice and worth considering as a prospecting philosophy. The principle, of course, is that the sensation of hunger will outweigh common sense and logic if you're not careful. If you go shopping while you're hungry, you may find that you arrived at the checkout counter with items in your cart that you don't need or that may not represent real value for you or your family. Why? Because you approached food selection from a "scarcity" mindset. "What can I eat right now?"

ABUNDANCE

What if you were to approach food shopping with a sense of abundance? If you were to go food shopping the day after Thanksgiving, having just consumed a big plate of leftovers from the annual American banquet, what would happen? My guess is you would probably end up with fewer items in your grocery cart than if you had returned from a week-long fishing trip where you did not catch many fish.

This same sense of abundance should apply to both your prospecting and sales efforts. If this seems unimaginable to you now, let me ask you a question. Pretend you have a pipeline chock-full of people who need your solution, who respect you as a peer and who have agreed to engage in your selling process versus their buying process. In that situation, how difficult would it be for an unqualified prospect to secure some of your selling time?

Now I realize that this is a bit of a catch-22. You might be saying to yourself, "I wish I had that problem. How can I act from a sense of abundance when I'm still trying to build my pipeline?"

Here's the paradox. Having a sense of abundance relating to sales is far more of a belief-system issue than it is an objective condition. If a brand-new salesperson started in your company tomorrow and had zero accounts in his pipeline, would he approach the pipeline-building effort with the mindset that says, "There are far more people who can buy from me than I have time in the day to call"? What salespeople in their right minds take a new position where they think they have less time in the day than prospects?

This advice I'm giving you about mindset may at first seem like a riddle. Perhaps it is, but if it is, it's worth solving. Early in my sales career, one of my managers noticed I was struggling with this concept. After observing how easy it was for an unqualified prospect to get an appointment with me, she said, "Do you know what your problem is, Rich? You're too nice!"

I was selling for IBM. The last thought that ever entered my mind was to avoid being too nice.

I also remember her telling me, "People cannot force you to sell to them." She meant that successful salespeople realize that they will come upon tire kickers, researchers and people doing pet projects. All of these folks have far more free time available than the salesperson. What would happen if you made it clear you would be submitting an hourly invoice whenever a meeting turned out to be a waste of your time? And that you expected it to be paid? If that were the agreement, these prospects would act a little differently.

SANDLER TIP

Ask yourself: Does this person have a demonstrated willingness and ability to move money and other resources around to fund a desired business outcome?

That manager taught me that in order to qualify, prospects must fulfill two critical criteria:

- First, they must have a business problem that is costing their company at least three times what your fully implemented solution will cost.
- Second, the individual to whom you're speaking must have a strong personal stake in seeing this problem go away and must be able to make it go away—or be willing to take you to the person who has those attributes.

How many of your current prospects meet those criteria?

It is not so much a question of whether they have a line item in their budget that will cover your solution. The question is whether they have a demonstrated willingness and ability to move money around to fund a desired business outcome.

THE "BUDGET" ISSUE

I do not believe I ever met a prospect who told me that he had already established a budget for sales training. Not one. Yet, I've sold a lot of sales training. I knew that if they needed the sales training to improve their business, they would find the money to cover my program, even if it meant taking it from a different project. The only catch was, the decision process I uncovered had to be reasonable and comparable in size and scope to the sales effort that would be involved. Fortunately, the beauty of finding the pain first is that anybody who is in a personal state of pain about a problem you can solve will typically provide you with all the data you need on both the budget and decision process.

THE "WHO'S LEADING THIS DANCE?" ISSUE

There was another critical point I learned that day from my manager at IBM. Even if people are qualified for pain, budget and decision, they may still not be a qualified prospect for your sales time. If they will not let you sell to them in a manner that historically has provided you with a high level of success, you should consider them disqualified. (This may or may not be evident in the first discussion, by the way.)

Will they try to dictate how you must sell? Will prospects try to put you in a permanent vendor status, or will they allow you to engage with them as a peer providing quid pro quo through mutual action plans? You need to be able to distinguish between these two types of prospects.

Nowhere is this professional selling obligation more important than in the situation where you are determining whether and how to respond to requests for proposals (RFPs). Anybody who has sold for a few years in the high-tech space is already aware of what terrible odds salespeople have of winning an RFP that they did not help the prospect create.

You're probably nodding your head right now. Here's something else you can nod your head to: Most experienced salespeople can readily identify which of their competitors got to the prospect first based upon the way the RFP is written. Features are clearly delineated with associated values, and all contact between any prospective vendors and the prospect is outlined within the RFP and cannot be modified or increased. When you read that, do you ever think it's a coincidence?

What's frustrating to many salespeople is that they can also see, just by reading the RFP, that their solution would be a great fit for the prospect's pain points. They also know that the budget dollars must be present, since the prospect devoted the time and cost necessary to create the RFP.

But what does any of that matter? The reality is that people make decisions to buy at an emotional level and then rationalize them with facts and data (even federal, state and local government accounts). Another salesperson got to this prospect before you did and, most likely, put the prospect in the pain state before you could. Whether we like it or not, that's what happened. This discussion moved the business problem from a back burner issue to a front burner issue in the prospect's mind and allowed the competitive salesperson to become the trusted advisor. The game is over.

So why should you even read this document? Usually because the procurement process of the prospect dictates that he must get at least three competitive bids before making a selection. The RFP needed to be created so that that there could be some (rigged) numerical scoring or ranking method that would allow the competitive salesperson's solution to come out on top. Not yours.

SELLER BEWARE

Now most salespeople are forewarned and forearmed about the perils of this whole RFP process. They learn quickly which RFPs, if any, they should take the time to complete. But they're not out of the woods. They still get manipulated. They still waste precious time.

What happens far more often is that "qualified" prospects want to engage with the salesperson on their own terms in their own fashion—and certainly not on a peer-to-peer basis. Every element of the RFP trap is still there, waiting to drain away the salesperson's most precious resource: time. Well, almost every element. All that is missing is the physical RFP document.

Prospects dictate to the salesperson what they want to see happen each and every step of the way. They tell the salesperson that unless he competes for the business on the prospects' terms, then they will take the salesperson off the "short list."

If your pipeline is empty, any prospect may seem like a good prospect. But if you engage with many prospects such as this, how will you ever have enough time to fill your pipeline with prospects who will let you sell to them in your preferred manner?

QUALIFYING, FOR REAL, WITH THE MUTUAL ACTION PLAN

A far better approach is to add one more step to your qualification process. Once the account is qualified for pain, budget and decision, ask the prospect if solving the business problem is something he would like to explore doing with you. If he is still in a state of personal pain, he is most likely going to agree and say "yes." This is where you secure a mutual action plan.

As discussed earlier, a "mutual action plan" (or MAP) is a fancy name for a mutually created strategy to get from where you are right now to the point in the future where the prospect tells you either, "Sorry, but you're not a good fit," or, "Send me a contract." It is a plan to make a decision.

Perhaps the easiest way to obtain this plan is to say something like the following:

May I make a suggestion? Would it make sense for you and me to outline all of the tasks we would have to complete in order to go from where we are now to either a *yes* or *no* decision? I'm looking through my notes, and I see that you have already agreed to contact the other stakeholders to verify the source of the budget dollars. I will provide you with some dates when we can meet with you and the other stakeholders and the contact information for two references. Now let's take a few minutes to think through all of the items, such as legal review of contract and ROI creation, and see if we can build a timeline of action items, responsibilities and duties.

What you are asking the prospect to do is collaborate in building a plan to arrive at a decision that involves both parties making an investment in terms of time and effort. That beats a "plan" where all the time and effort come from your side.

You cannot ask for a plan that guarantees that the prospect will buy from you, but it is perfectly reasonable to ask for help creating a plan by which the prospect can arrive at a decision. This is where the experienced salesperson also solidifies the communication agreement by utilization of the "biggest fear" technique. It might sound something like this:

I really appreciate you building out our plan in such detail. But, there is one thing that sometimes happens in other accounts. I'm not sure that it will happen here, but I feel like I should mention it. Sometimes when we're working with clients creating these action plans, the problem we're solving has the highest priority at that time. Then as the plan progresses, priorities sometimes change, and our project might go on the back burner. If that were to happen here, can I count on you just to let me know?

By obtaining this commitment from the prospect, the salesperson has not only created a MAP that ensures the sales process occurs in a way that will most favor his solution, but has also secured an agreement from the prospect not to "go dark" on the salesperson should other priorities arise.

Let's go back to the example where the prospect did not issue an RFP but wanted the salesperson to engage in what might be called an RFP-like manner. If your current day was full of working prospects in which you had secured a MAP and there were now two new prospects vying for your attention, how would you decide which was the highest priority? Well, if one was the "RFP-like" prospect and the other was one who would agree to your MAP communication agreement, isn't the choice obvious?

Remember, you can get to a pipeline full of qualified prospects who will engage with you in your preferred manner, but only if you believe that you can get there from where you are today.

KEY TAKEAWAYS

- All qualified prospects must fulfill two critical criteria:
  - First, they must have a business problem that is costing their company at least three times what your fully implemented solution will cost.
  - Second, the individual to whom you're speaking must have a strong personal stake in seeing this problem go away and must be able to make it go away or be willing to take you to the person who can.
- A "sense of abundance" means that you have far more people to sell to than you have time for in your day. Don't be so quick to enter unilateral sales engagements in which you are not treated as an equal.

CHAPTER 11

Handling Objections

D id you ever stop to consider how many big choices you've made to get to this point in your life? Stop and think for a moment about all the major decisions you've made in the moments leading up to right now.

In all likelihood, you have decided on whom to marry, where to work, where to live and scores of other major life issues. After you created your shortlist for each of these major choices, did you have many serious questions or doubts about which should be your final selection? Most people say "no."

Additionally, it's likely that any alternatives you eliminated early in the cycle never had a chance to answer any of your concerns. After all, if you didn't like where the house was located, what difference does it make whether the current mortgage was assumable? If the manager you would be working for completely turned you off in the first interview, would you ask questions about the benefits package?

Sometimes salespeople forget that prospects are people— people who make decisions in the same way they do. What do I mean by that? The absence of questions or objections halfway through your presentation isn't always good news. It usually indicates that the prospect doesn't consider you to be a finalist. These prospects don't feel they need the detail from you that would be required from those they are taking seriously as a solution provider. The overriding big message for this chapter is simple—objections are a salesperson's best friend.

SANDLER TIP

If you are new with your company, ask the more experienced salespeople what you should expect and what tools exist to assist you in addressing the most common objections.

Whether you are a deal chaser or relationship builder, you'll probably agree that the one part of the salesperson's job that can throw you off your game is handling objections. For some reason this seems to be the aspect of the sales cycle for which salespeople prepare the least. As a result, it's the area with which they're the least comfortable. The lack of preparedness usually increases the salesperson's anxiety when objections arise.

Reality check: After you have been selling any solution for

six months or so, you will probably have heard most of the objections you will ever hear with regard to your solution. After all, there are only so many objections out there. If you are new to a company, ask the more experienced salespeople what you should expect and what tools exist to assist you in addressing these objections.

The good news is that there are three simple keys to successfully handling objections:

1. Handle your own anxiety.
2. Understand the real objection.
3. Defuse the prospect's emotion and put him back into a receptive mode.

HANDLING THE ANXIETY

Some salespeople would rather get a wisdom tooth pulled than sit with a prospect and handle objections. For some, this anxiety comes from their belief that a good salesperson eliminates all of the tension in the sales cycle. They view objections to price, features and anything else as a challenge to the sales tranquility they are trying to create.

One of the biggest mistakes that high-tech salespeople can make is to believe that they should eliminate all tension. The skillful use of tension is essential during the qualifying stage, the fulfillment stage and, perhaps most importantly, during the negotiation stage of your sales cycle.

Remember: Objections typically mean that you have moved forward from that early stage of being an interruption to the

more desired stage of consideration. If you agree with this statement, then you should be more anxious when you don't get objections than you are when you do.

Another reason some salespeople get anxious when dealing
with objections is that they take any question or negative statement from the prospect as a personal insult. When prospects say,
"You must be kidding!" when they hear the price, the salesperson hears them say, "You are not worth this amount of money."

Salespeople trained in the Sandler methodology learn early
how to separate their identity from their role as a salesperson.
Remember from our prospecting chapter: When prospects hang
up on your cold call, they aren't rejecting you as a person. You
may have only gotten six words out of your mouth before they
realized it was a cold call. They simply did not want to speak to
anyone. If you don't realize that it was your role as a cold caller
that they rejected rather than yourself, you may ask, "What's
wrong with me?" Either way, the answer is, "Nothing."

If your friends and relatives consistently hang up on you before you get a half-dozen words out, you might need to do some
soul-searching. But when people question or raise objections
about your company or your solution, you need to recognize
that they are providing you with an opportunity to sell to them
and not making a personal attack.

I've been selling for over 30 years, and I never once remember telling a prospect how much something cost and getting the
reply, "Is that all? I thought it would be far more expensive!"
Seriously, any price greater than zero places the prospect in the
role of trying to get a lower price and places the salesperson in

the role of maintaining the price. That's the game. It's all about role-playing, so please don't take it personally.

WHAT'S THE REAL OBJECTION?

Similar to what often happens in the Pain Step, sometimes prospects have trouble articulating (and we have trouble hearing) the real objection. This means that you need to own a repeatable process by which you can use active listening and reversing to understand the prospect's real objection.

Remember, it's probable that you carry some baggage from prospect to prospect. You can easily cause more damage than good by answering the objection you believe you heard instead of identifying the one the prospect was trying to articulate. Let me give you a real life example of this. When I was SVP of global sales for a large enterprise software company, we regularly met with Fortune 500 companies to create multiyear proposals. These were worth $20–$50 million per year, so our sales force was preconditioned for the objection of price.

At one meeting with a large insurance company, the CIO said that he had reviewed our proposal and had a problem with our contract. My sales VP cut him off and started to defend our pricing almost as a reflex. As it turned out, the CIO's problem was not with the price but with the ability to move our products from existing to future data centers. Had my sales VP taken the time to understand what the problem with the contract was rather than assuming that it must be price, he would have saved both of us considerable misery.

The moral of the story: Assume nothing. Answer a question with a question, using the Sandler concept known as reversing. (For instance: "That's a great question. And you're asking it because...?") Be prepared to pose questions repeatedly until you get to the bottom of things. Use techniques such as active listening, where you say back to the prospect what you think you heard, as a way of confirming the true objection.

DEFUSE THE EMOTION

The third key to handling objections is to absorb the objection, thereby defusing any of the prospect's emotion.

An experienced sales professional is adept at viewing the objection from the prospect's point of view, rather than from the vendor's point of view. Sandler calls this "getting to the same side of the desk" as the prospect. You can use this technique to address just about any objection.

The first step is to listen all the way through the objection and never to cut the person off because you believe you know where it is going. How do you feel when you're complaining to someone at a store and the person behind the counter cuts you off? You resent it, I bet, even if the interruption is the start of an apology.

The next step requires you to play back to the prospect what you believe you heard and get him to confirm that you understand the real objection. If multiple objections are being tossed your way, you will need to isolate and prioritize each objection. No one can effectively address multiple objections in the same thought track.

Next comes the most important step. Using the same approach a nurturing parent might use, you need to agree with how the person feels. This doesn't mean that you agree with the objection, but rather that you let him know that in his situation, you would probably feel the same way.

The last thing you ever want to tell someone with an objection is, "You know, you really shouldn't feel that way." (If you do not believe me, try saying that the next time your significant other is in the middle of informing you about something that you did wrong.)

SANDLER TIP

Viewing the objection from the prospect's point of view quickly puts you on the same side of the desk as your prospect.

An example: Let's say you're on the phone with a prospect you are trying to qualify for the Budget Step and you give a ballpark price. The prospect indicates that the figure is far higher than expected. You could respond with something like this:

If I were you I'd feel the same way. I mean, you and I have only spoken for about ten minutes and all of a sudden we are discussing spending a serious amount of money. On the other hand, since our company is growing so rapidly, there must be many companies out there that value and need our service. Would it make sense for us to continue our conversation to see if you might become one of those companies?

This combination of a nurturing parent's approach, followed by a logical, adult assessment of the situation, quickly puts the salesperson on the same side of the desk as the prospect.

In the fourth step of our process, you attempt to ascertain the source of the objection. Did your prospect think of this objection on his own, or was the idea planted by your competition? Your best first response is always a question, such as, "You must be telling me that for a reason—which is...?" This will help you understand the extent to which the prospect believes in the objection as well as the source of the information.

When the prospect has trouble articulating the nature of the objection and its impact on his company, this is a clear sign that the objection came from someone else. Don't worry, this is great! Most objections are not well-rooted and are tossed out to salespeople by prospects who are trying to test them. For example, let's say that you are competing for the sale against a much larger company. That competitor always tells your joint prospects that they should be worrying about your company's financial viability. The prospect may not believe your viability is an issue, but they will toss the objection out to see how you handle it. If you handle the question calmly and smoothly, telling the prospect that you hear that a lot and outlining all the reasons he should dismiss this issue, then the objection will go away. On the other hand, if you are unprepared for this objection and break out into a cold sweat with an unconvincing, rambling answer, you will probably cement in this prospect's mind that your financial viability really is a problem.

SANDLER TIP

Since most objections are not well-rooted, you must be capable of addressing the objection immediately.

Since most objections are not well-rooted, you must be capable of addressing the objection immediately. Once you have provided the prospect with your answer, you need to confirm that he is comfortable with your response. Something as simple as, "Did I address your concern?" is usually all it takes for you to determine whether the objection has been addressed, requires more attention or is a potential showstopper. If the prospect tells you that he is comfortable with your response, you are now able to redirect the conversation back into your story line.

SANDLER TIP

Not every objection can be surmounted. If a key buying requirement for the prospect is something you can't provide, disqualify the prospect. Don't waste any more time on this or subsequent sales calls.

Some objections require additional actions from the salesperson after the current meeting. The issue of financial viability may require you to provide the prospect with audited bank statements or a conversation with your chief financial officer. You should be able to ask the prospect the following question: "Assuming I provide you with our audited financials and an opportunity to speak with our CFO, will that allay your concerns?" If the prospect agrees, then you can press ahead with your sales call.

Not every objection can be surmounted. This is part of the qualification process. If your prospect has a big manufacturing center in Poland, management may object to doing business with any vendor that does not have local support in Poland. When they ask you about your firm's support in that country and your answer is, "We don't have any," you probably need to ask the prospect whether this is a showstopper.

If a key buying requirement for a prospect is something you cannot provide, why waste any more time on this or subsequent sales calls? This is one of the great values of handling objections properly. You get to move qualified prospects further into your sales cycle while moving unqualified prospects off your calendar.

KEY TAKEAWAYS

- Objections are your friends. No one makes a buying decision without raising some objections.
- When handling an objection, always agree with how the person feels but not necessarily the objection itself.
- One of the biggest mistakes you can make is to believe your role is to eliminate all tension within the sales cycle. The skillful use of tension is essential during the qualifying stage, the fulfillment stage and, perhaps most importantly, during the negotiation stage of your sales cycle.

CHAPTER 12

More on Mutual Action Plans

W ho among us cannot recall a significant deal in which both the prospect and ourselves started out the sales cycle with great enthusiasm, only to have the prospect's energy dwindle and die out? If we are honest about critiquing our own sales efforts, we might find that we did not properly capitalize on the prospect's emotional "peak."

History tells us the best approach in pursuing the last two-thirds of any sales cycle is to create a joint project plan that contains action items and due dates for both the prospect and the sales team. These are sometimes referred to as a quid pro quo, a joint pursuit plan or, as discussed earlier, a mutual action plan (MAP). This technique is worth examining in depth because it usually provides the salesperson with two significant benefits.

First, it ensures that both you and the prospect are creating a joint effort and using project management skills to manage tasks and timelines. Second, it provides you, the salesperson, with a valuable tool to discover early on whether this is a "sanctioned" project by the prospect's company or a "research" project authorized by one person only. To understand why this approach is so effective, consider the following.

> ### SANDLER TIP
> *Create a mutual action plan with action items and due dates for people on both sides of the desk.*

From the salesperson's perspective, having a fully qualified prospect at the table seems like a dream come true. Sometimes salespeople are so excited by the potential commission that they feel it is their duty to complete all of the tasks still required. Asking the prospect to assume any action item burden might scare them off. This is when the deal becomes "my deal" (the salesperson's) versus "our deal."

Their enthusiasm has made them overlook the fact that to be fully qualified for the Budget Step, a prospect must be willing to invest time and effort as well as budget dollars in the pursuit of the proposed solution. If the salesperson assumes all of the actions, that allows the prospect to both physically and emotionally disengage from the sales process.

Let's look at it from the prospect's perspective. Assume I'm the prospect. The salesperson got my attention at the initial meeting, but I had other priorities on my plate at that time. When I informed the salesperson of this fact, the reply was, "Don't worry, I will take care of everything." From my point of view, if the salesperson wants to chase after this project, that's up to him.

Given these two very different points of view, is it any wonder that the salesperson feels like he's "pushing a rope"? This situation typically culminates when the sales manager starts questioning the time and effort that has been expended on this prospect by the salesperson—at about the same time the prospect stops returning ever-increasing requests for status updates from the salesperson.

> ## SANDLER TIP
>
> *After uncovering the personal pain of any prospect, the next question should always be, "Is this something worth pursuing?"*

The salesperson should have created a MAP with the prospect at qualification time prior to beginning the remainder of the sales process. After uncovering the personal pain of any prospect, the next question should always be, "Is this something worth pursuing?"

If the prospect says "yes," you have been "invited in." It is at this point you may say something like:

May I make a suggestion? Would it make sense for you and me to make a list of all the action items that both of us would need to complete in order to arrive at either a *no, thanks* or a *yes, we want to move forward with you* decision?

If you uncovered his personal pain, you are far more likely to gain his involvement in this effort. You will be creating an "our deal" mindset. If the prospect starts to balk at assuming any action items, you should take this as a big red flag that you have not uncovered enough personal pain.

Why do I emphasize this? Why does it deserve a chapter all its own? Because if you're not solving a big enough problem to make the prospect do some effort in assessing your solution, you are certainly not solving a big enough problem to make this prospect ask for the money and put his neck on the line. Also, remember an earlier question I asked: "How many of your prospects would call you if you stopped calling them?" If you were engaged only with prospects who were executing against a MAP, I can assure you that most of these prospects would call you if you stopped calling them. By agreeing to a MAP, they have indicated they need to buy from you as much as you need to sell to them. That is why they would come looking for you.

In any given sales cycle, there may be different project plans based on what you are selling and the financial size of the transaction. Typically the salesperson's action items will include such steps as: interviewing stakeholders, setting up a demo, structuring a proof of concept, providing a proposal, furnishing references and introducing the post-sales team. The prospect's list of tasks might include: introducing you to the stakeholders, providing data for the demo, giving you access to their ROI requirements, having their legal department review your contract, introducing the salesperson's executives to the prospect's executives and increasing visibility within the company as the sales cycle progresses in a positive manner. This MAP approach will also provide the prospect with a graceful way to go back and fact-check some of the data that was provided to the salesperson during the qualification phase. For example, can the prospect move budget dollars from one line item to another? Did the prospect identify all of the stakeholders? And so on.

I pointed out earlier that this approach will also protect the salesperson from being part of a research project for a prospect who does not have the authority to purchase a solution. Experience dictates that any sizable acquisition of new technology, especially one that introduces a new vendor company, will have the prospect's management wanting to meet with vendor management. Highly successful high-tech salespeople understand this concept and are adept at aligning layers of their own management in subsequent meetings with the prospect's management as part of the normal sales cycle progression.

They do this "executive bridging" for two reasons. First, it enables the salesperson to create a more accurate forecast date while setting the stage for the inevitable price negotiation. Additionally, experienced salespeople have seen firsthand that prospects will give different answers to a question from the salesperson's executive than was provided to the salesperson on the very same question. As such, salespeople should refuse to engage in a

6–12 month sales cycle in which they stay compartmentalized within the prospect's organizational structure.

Successful sales managers also recognize that having their introduction into the sales cycle at the appropriate time enables them to leverage their time and skills with their forecasted opportunities. This is especially true when the salesperson's company has invested a significant amount of time and effort at no charge to the prospect.

SANDLER TIP

Truly qualified prospects should no more want to waste their time than salespeople would want to waste their own time.

Let me share a story that illustrates this point. Once when I was doing a forecast review with my sales team, I questioned why we had invested so many work days into an opportunity with a Fortune 500 company without obtaining an executive meeting. Since I was senior VP of sales, I felt that the CIO would not be offended by my reaching out to him via the telephone. The CIO took my call and was shocked to discover that someone on his team had invested so much time in a clearly unsanctioned project. His exact words—which I remember to this day—were, "We have had so many budget cuts that we can barely pay for what we have already in place. Even our toilet paper is here on consignment!" Needless to say, we stopped the sales cycle. But the salesperson had wasted four months with this unqualified opportunity.

The lesson here is that truly qualified prospects should no more want to waste their time than salespeople would want to waste their own time. The prospect still keeps his "day job" while attending the salesperson's meetings, demonstrations, etc. Most qualified prospects will want to make the right decision as quickly as possible so they can go back to doing their day job full time. As such, when the salesperson introduces the MAP concept and volunteers to be the project manager (as opposed to simply doing all of the tasks), the prospect will typically view this very favorably. Presenting this option is essential because it secures for you the role of trusted advisor. Of course, that's where you want to be.

As a prospect once told me, "Makes sense to me. After all, you do this every day, and I have only done this once before."

Yes, he ended up buying from me.

KEY TAKEAWAYS

- You have lived through many sales cycles for your solution, but this is probably the first time for the prospect. You are the subject matter expert on both buying and selling.

- Getting "invited in" by the prospect makes a big difference in your ability to control the sales cycle.

- The best approach in pursuing the last two-thirds of any sales cycle is to create a joint project plan that contains action items and due dates for both the prospect and the sales team. This makes it "our deal"!

EPILOGUE

I f I had shared everything in these pages that I share in person with my clients, this book could have been easily three times as long. I suppose there's no way to pack into a single book all of the experience, all of the disappointment, all of the triumph, that comes along with selling for a living in the high-tech space. What I have tried to do is share with you the most essential points necessary for success in our field, in a format that is as accessible and concise as I would have wanted to read if I were starting from scratch. I hope I've succeeded.

Most of what I've shared comes from the Sandler Selling System, of course, and all of what I've written here has been confirmed through direct personal experience. I hope it has been helpful to you, and I look forward to hearing directly from you about your experiences in implementing the program I've laid out here.

—Rich Chiarello

Look for these other books
on Amazon.com:

Prospect the Sandler Way

Transforming Leaders the Sandler Way

Selling Professional Services the Sandler Way

Accountability the Sandler Way

CONGRATULATIONS!

Selling Technology the Sandler Way

includes a complimentary seminar!

Take this opportunity to personally experience the non-traditional sales training and reinforcement coaching that has been recognized internationally for decades.

Companies in the Fortune 1000 as well as thousands of small- to medium-sized businesses choose Sandler Training for sales, leadership, management, and a wealth of other skill-building programs. Now, it's your turn, and it's free!

You'll learn the latest practical, tactical, feet-in-the-street sales methods directly from your neighborhood Sandler trainers! They're knowledgeable, friendly and informed about your local selling environment.

Here's how you redeem YOUR FREE SEMINAR invitation.

1. Go to www.Sandler.com and click on the LOCATE A TRAINING CENTER button (upper right corner).
2. Select your location from the drop-down menus.
3. Review the list of all the Sandler trainers in your area.
4. Call your local Sandler trainer, mention *Selling Technology the Sandler Way* and reserve your place at the next seminar!